STOKED

6 Questions To Fuel
Your Fire For Jesus

Stoked

6 Questions To Fuel Your Fire For Jesus

CHASE SNYDER

Loganville, Georgia

Copyright © 2018 CHASE SNYDER

All rights are reserved. No part of this publication can be reproduced or copied in any way without the expressed written consent of 228 Publishers and the author. This book was written, printed, and designed in the United States of America.

ISBN: 0-9984876-1-9
ISBN-13: 978-0-9984876-1-8

All Scripture quotations, unless otherwise indicated, are taken from the Holy Bible, New International Version, NIV. Copyright ©1973, 1978, 1984, 2011 by Biblica, Inc. Used by permission of Zondervan. All rights reserved worldwide.
www.zondervan.com The "NIV" and "New International Version" are trademarks registered in the United States Patent and Trademark Office by Biblica, Inc.

228 Publishers
Loganville, Georgia
www.228Publishers.com
228 Publishers is a Division of Ministry Bubble LLC

228 Publishers President and Publisher: Anne Snyder
Cover and Layout Design: Chase Snyder

Copies of this book are available to churches, schools, and small groups at a significant quantity discount. For more details, go to **www.228Publishers.com**.

To my incredible wife and two kids. Anne, Tripp, and Brooke, you continually stoke my passion for Jesus.

I pray that I am leading and teaching you to stoke your passions for Jesus. God has incredible plans for your lives. May your passions burn brightly and powerfully for Jesus.

Table of Contents

Start Here   1

Week 1   5
What Is Extinguishing My Passion for Jesus?

Week 2   25
Who Is Stoking My Passion for Jesus?

Week 3   49
What Is God Teaching Me through His Word?

Week 4   71
What Is Consuming My Thoughts and Time?

Week 5   93
How Has Jesus Shown Up in My Life This Week?

Week 6   115
Who Am I Bringing Closer to Jesus?

Continue to Fan the Flame   136

About the Author   137

Additional Resources   138

Start Here

A fire needs three elements for it to burn.

It needs fuel to consume.
It needs oxygen to breathe.
It needs a spark to ignite.

A fire will go out if you take any of these three elements away. Stop adding logs, and the fire will burn out. Take away the oxygen, and the fire will suffocate. Don't strike the match, and the tinder sits alone without a flame.

It isn't rocket science to keep a campfire going. But anyone who has tried to build a fire knows that it isn't as easy as it seems. Even with three variables and a straightforward process, many have to add something extra to keep it going. Some are quick to grab a bottle of lighter fluid or kerosene to stoke a fire. (By the way, that's seen as cheating in the outdoor community, unless it creates an awesome fireball!)

In Christian circles, it's common to hear statements about being "on fire" for Jesus. It's a way of saying that someone is close to Jesus, passionate about their faith, or generally in a good place spiritually.

Too many times, I've seen that fire for Jesus start to burn out. I hear the same questions every time: "Why does God feel distant?" "How can I get closer to Jesus?" "Why am I not on fire for God anymore?"

This book will talk about building and maintaining your spiritual fire. I call that stoking your fire for Jesus.

Can you be honest with yourself for a minute? Ask yourself this one question:

Has there been a time when your fire for Jesus was burning hotter than it is right now?

If so, I invite you on a six-week spiritual journey to discover what is trying to extinguish your spiritual fire and how to stoke your passion for Jesus.

Two Ways to Use This Book

On Your Own

This book will take you on a journey to stoke your fire for Jesus. It's best to read it over the course of six weeks. Each week starts with a session that explains the focus question for that week. The session is a short chapter that ends with a passage to study and questions to answer. Read the session as the first day's study. There are five devotions following the main session, which gives you six days of content per week. The devotions are short and designed for engagement with God's Word.

In a Small Group

You can also use this book as curriculum for a small group. This is great for creating accountability for yourself. Using this book with others will deepen the impact of the spiritual truths you will learn.

Each week has one main session for you to discuss during your weekly group gathering. Use the passage to study and questions to answer to spark spiritual conversations. Group members can complete the daily devotions during the week and discuss them at meetings.

Each Daily Devotion Includes

Daily Scripture

Each daily Scripture relates to the week's main question. I encourage you to open your Bible and read the verses surrounding the daily Scripture. The more time you spend in the Bible during the next six weeks, the deeper your studies will be. You'll gain an understanding of the context of each verse or passage, and you will see God move in your life.

Daily Devotional Reading

A daily devotional thought follows each Scripture passage. These devotions will get you thinking about the week's topic more deeply. The devotions also cover key concepts from the Scripture provided.

Daily Application

To the right of the daily devotion is a section for you to practice applying that Scripture to your life. To stoke your fire for Jesus, you must apply the Scripture you are reading.

You'll answer the same six questions each day for six weeks. You'll be surprised by how different your answers will be based on the Scripture passages you read.

Even though you will be repeating these questions every day, you will love the results. Your answers will vary greatly based on the different Scripture passages. And you will learn how to read, interpret, and apply Scripture methodically.

This page has three sections: Upward, Inward, and Outward. Under each section you will find two questions to answer and pray through.

Upward – Focus on God
The Bible is the very Word of God, so the first section deals with looking upward to Him. These questions point you to what the passage shows you about God. You'll notice new characteristics and promises to take hold of.

Inward – Personal Application
There is only one interpretation of Scripture (the actual meaning of the passage or verse). But there can be many applications to your life and situation. As you read the Bible, you'll start to see areas of your heart that are in need of God's grace, love, or correction. These questions ask you what the biblical passage reveals about your habits and heart.

Outward – Live It Out
The last section focuses on your active response to the passage you've studied. Some days you will need to seek out others to serve them or share the Gospel of Jesus. It is possible that you might need to commit to a new habit or have a conversation with a friend. The Outward section focuses on how you will live out what you believe. These questions will direct you to practically apply biblical truth to your life and stoke your fire for Jesus.

WEEK 1

WHAT IS EXTINGUISHING MY PASSION FOR JESUS?

Week 1 – Day 1

What Is Extinguishing My Passion for Jesus?

We are quick to finish the statement "Things will be better when ..." with all kinds of hypothetical circumstances.

Things will be better when I have more money.
Things will be better when I have a different job.
Things will be better when I graduate and get out of here.
Things will be better when I get a degree.
Things will be better when I lose weight.
Things will be better when I have better friends.

But those hypotheticals aren't the solution to make your life better.

Nothing in these statements will bring us lasting joy, comfort, and peace. Instead, the seemingly "perfect" circumstances we seek out will leave us wanting more. Only Jesus will make things better.

When was the last time you had one of these thoughts?

Spending more time with Jesus will make things better.
Confessing my sin to Jesus will make things better.
Obeying Jesus will make things better.

Have you ever noticed how quickly we run to everything else and leave Jesus as a last resort? *Nothing will fuel our lives and stoke our spiritual fires like Jesus.*

Secure in the Family

When you commit your life to Jesus and repent of your sins, the Bible says you enter the family of God. That's something a Christian never loses. Jesus Himself promised that.

Jesus said in John 10:28-29, "I give them eternal life, and they shall never perish; no one will snatch them out of my hand. My Father, who has given them to me, is greater than all; no one can snatch them out of my Father's hand."

This isn't a book about earning your salvation; earning your salvation is impossible. Ephesians 2:8-10 explains, "For it is by grace you have been saved, through faith—and this is not from yourselves, it is the gift of God—not by works, so that no one can boast. For we are God's handiwork, created in Christ Jesus to do good works, which God prepared in advance for us to do."

Your salvation is secure. But your passion can burn out if you don't stoke your spiritual fire.

All Fires Can Burn Out

When I was a kid, my family would go camping at a nearby lake. For us, camping was a mixture of sleeping in an RV and roughing it in a tent. My parents usually slept in the RV, but my brother, sister, and I would beg to sleep in the tent.

One night, my dad almost caught our tent on fire.

It was an unfortunate accident, for sure. He left a citronella candle burning until we fell asleep. When he got up to blow out the candle, he discovered that the oil had completely burned up. The candle was boiling and burning like a grease fire.

Half asleep and shocked by the small fire in front of him, he did the first thing that came to mind – he threw water on the candle. But citronella candles and water do not mix. As soon as the water hit the boiling oil, a ten-foot-tall fire bomb exploded right next to our tent. Luckily, our tent didn't catch on fire, and my dad was able to extinguish the fire before it spread.

That experience taught me at a young age that there are specific ways to extinguish fires. In fact, there are five different classes of fire extinguishers used to put out different types of fires, depending on what materials are present.

Just like real fires are put out in specific ways, there are specific reasons why your passion for Jesus is burning out.

Think back to a time when you experienced closeness with God.

Perhaps during a camp you experienced a closeness with God that you had never felt before. You saw Jesus move in real ways in your life during the week.

You read your Bible.
Temptations were minimal.
Spiritual conversations were plentiful.
You worshipped Jesus day and night.
Friendships with other Christians were strengthened.

Everything was going well ... until you went home.

You went back to your normal schedule.
Your friends didn't affirm the new you.
Old struggles crept back into your life.
Sinful habits once again became second nature.

And just like that, you no longer felt the closeness with God that you experienced while away at a spiritual retreat.

What happened? Did Jesus somehow change between the time you left the retreat center and your arrival at home? Did you make promises to God in vain? Were you caught up in the emotion of camp? Did your pastor not do enough to prepare you for coming back to the real world?

Nope. I don't believe that any of these are the true reason that your fire started burning out. Jesus didn't change. Your commitments were genuine. Your church wants you to grow. So, what happened?

Busy Isn't Better

Somewhere along the way, you filled your schedule with things that distracted you from Jesus instead of bringing you closer to Him. Somewhere along the way, your eyes shifted from Jesus to day-to-day responsibilities.

The semester gets busy and you don't have time for anything but studying. The season is starting so you add a few extra practices in each week. You want some extra spending money so you pick up a side job after class.

School, sports, and side jobs aren't evil, but they bring shifts in our schedules and thinking that pose a dangerous threat to our spiritual lives if we aren't holding tightly to Jesus. If you aren't careful, you will become so busy that you will become distracted and lose focus on Jesus. Once we take our eyes off Jesus, we start searching for a replacement. We look for love, acceptance, identity, and comfort. Jesus is the ultimate giver of life; distracted living causes our eyes and hearts to wander.

Your spiritual fire will grow as a result of prioritizing the correct things. If you prioritize the wrong things, your spiritual fire will fizzle out. You'll become more busy with worldly things and less busy with godly things.

Christians don't set out to become so busy that they allow their fire for Jesus to burn out. But I've seen it over and over again.

It isn't that we want to ignore Jesus – our priorities simply shift away from Jesus and onto something lesser.

We simply get distracted.

Turn Away from Worthless Things

Psalm 119:37 says, "Turn my eyes away from worthless things; preserve my life according to your word."

Even though Psalm 119 was written a long time ago, worthless things haven't disappeared. They are all around us.

Right now you might be wondering what part of your day I would consider worthless. Your day is probably packed with school, work, and activities that have to get done. And I bet most of the things you do all day are productive and purposeful.

So what does the Psalmist mean by "worthless things"?

Something is worthless if it fails to bring you closer to Jesus. And many productive and purposeful activities fail that test.

Here are some examples of worthless things you may encounter. Some will be obvious, and some won't.

Sin is worthless. It's the No. 1 extinguisher of our passion for Jesus. Guilt creeps in and pulls us away from our Savior, and our passion for Him fades with every sin we purposefully commit. God commands us to resist temptation and flee sin so we can live passionately for Jesus.

Busy schedules are worthless. In an attempt to do *everything*, we miss doing what is *necessary*. If you are too busy, too tired, and too committed to spend time focusing on God, your schedule fails to bring you closer to God. Heaven isn't full of high achievers. Heaven is full of Jesus-followers.

Bad influences are worthless. If a relationship extinguishes your fire for Jesus, you may need to walk away from it. Some influences you allow into your life are great, and you should embrace them. But some pull you away from Jesus. Those are the relationships that need to be evaluated and/or removed.

Worthless things show up in a variety of ways. They often promise to bring life, security, and success. The true test is whether they bring us closer to Jesus or leave us feeling empty and separated from Jesus. *Something is worthless if it fails to bring you closer to Jesus.*

If you can't decide if something fails to bring you closer to Jesus, you may be tempted to label it as "neutral" and move on.

In the Bible, Paul offers a way to distinguish between what is worth our time and what is worthless. Philippians 4:8 says, "Finally, brothers and sisters, whatever is true, whatever is noble, whatever is right, whatever is pure, whatever is lovely, whatever is admirable—if anything is excellent or praiseworthy—think about such things."

This verse offers a powerful aim for your spiritual life. Focus on what honors Jesus by testing your activities, relationships, tasks, and thoughts on those attributes.

What Is Extinguishing My Passion for Jesus?

The question for this week is this: *What is extinguishing your passion for Jesus?*

You probably already know the answer to that question.

If you don't right away, think it over. What is different between how you go about your day now and how you operated at a time when you felt closer to God?

You can't stoke a fire if you are throwing water on it at the same time. You may need to make some changes.

Turn from worthless things.
Set your eyes on Jesus.
Repent of your sins.
Throw off everything that is hindering you.
Talk with your small group about your struggles.

It's time to stoke your passion for Jesus.

Now What?

Passage to Study: Romans 6:1-14

Questions:
1. What "worthless things" are causing your passion for Jesus to burn out?
2. What is your definition of sin?
3. Even though sin is no longer our master, why do we feel controlled by it?

Week 1 – Day 2

1 John 1:8-9 – "If we claim to be without sin, we deceive ourselves and the truth is not in us. If we confess our sins, he is faithful and just and will forgive us our sins and purify us from all unrighteousness."

To reignite your spiritual fire, you must admit to God, yourself, and others that you are not perfect. It's OK to admit that you have sinned. In fact, it's necessary.

Chances are, you have felt the temptation to portray your life as better and more put together than it is. But that is being fake. You aren't perfect. Keeping up a fake life is tough work that produces stress, doubt, and insecurity.

That isn't the way Jesus intends for us to live. We are all broken and in need of Jesus' forgiveness and love. Acknowledging your sin to God, as today's verses instruct, helps you stoke your passion for Jesus. It must be a habit you perform daily, because sin is an everyday occurrence.

This is God's promise to us: Jesus is willing to forgive our past sins and invite us on a journey with Him. Through the cross, Jesus has made a way for us to walk in His forgiving grace. He wants our passions to burn brightly for Him.

Week 1 – Day 2 Applied

Upward – Focus on God
What does today's passage tell you about God's character, promises, plans, or heart?

What attitude or emotion should that spark in you?

Inward – Personal Application
What does this passage reveal about your habits, attitude, and heart?

Is there an attitude you need to change, action you need to take, or sin you need to turn from?

Outward – Live It Out
What is the next step you must take to live out the truth of today's passage?

When and how will you take that step?

Week 1 – Day 3

Proverbs 14:12 – "There is a way that appears to be right, but in the end it leads to death."

Have you ever thought you were right about something, only to find out that you were completely wrong? That feeling stings, doesn't it?

Proverbs 14:12 warns us that sometimes what seems right at first isn't the best decision. That's because we are all born with a sin nature, so our first instinct isn't always the best one. We may think something will lead to prosperity, but instead it could lead to emptiness.

This gets to the very core of the problem with all the worthless things we allow into our lives. If a habit, action, commitment, or influence is worthless, it will lead us away from Jesus. If we continue to give it our devotion, it will extinguish our passion for Jesus.

The fight against worthless things like sin, busyness, and bad influences requires action! You must make an effort to stoke your fire for Jesus (like you are doing right now). If you do, you will experience more and more closeness with Jesus.

Week 1 – Day 3 Applied

Upward – Focus on God
What does today's passage tell you about God's character, promises, plans, or heart?

What attitude or emotion should that spark in you?

Inward – Personal Application
What does this passage reveal about your habits, attitude, and heart?

Is there an attitude you need to change, action you need to take, or sin you need to turn from?

Outward – Live It Out
What is the next step you must take to live out the truth of today's passage?

When and how will you take that step?

Week 1 – Day 4

James 4:8 – "Come near to God and he will come near to you. Wash your hands, you sinners, and purify your hearts, you double-minded."

When our spiritual fire isn't burning brightly, Jesus can seem far away. But Jesus isn't distant or unattached. He is active in His creation, including in your everyday life.

God's Word makes it clear that as we draw near to Him, He will draw near to us. God loves you, and He desires to have a friendship with you.

You *can* draw nearer to God than you are right now, even if it seems difficult. A great start is to identify what is causing you to drift away.

Identifying the root of your spiritual burnout may be painful. Sin wants to remain a stronghold in your life. It will not let go without a fight!

Thankfully, our strength to fight spiritual battles comes from Jesus. Draw near to the One who loves you most. He will show you what is causing you to drift away from Him, and He will help you overcome it.

Week 1 – Day 4 Applied

Upward – Focus on God
What does today's passage tell you about God's character, promises, plans, or heart?

What attitude or emotion should that spark in you?

Inward – Personal Application
What does this passage reveal about your habits, attitude, and heart?

Is there an attitude you need to change, action you need to take, or sin you need to turn from?

Outward – Live It Out
What is the next step you must take to live out the truth of today's passage?

When and how will you take that step?

Week 1 – Day 5

James 5:16 – "Therefore confess your sins to each other and pray for each other so that you may be healed. The prayer of a righteous person is powerful and effective."

Have you ever tried to move a couch by yourself? It is extremely difficult for one person to move such a large object alone. At best, you are able to pick up one side and pivot the beast a few inches closer to the new location. Don't even think about carrying a full-size couch up a flight of stairs by yourself! Carrying something that large requires more than one person.

In the same way, experiencing passion for the things of God requires more than just you. Before you knew Christ, you may have tried to do life on your own. If you try that approach while following Jesus, you will experience hardship.

You would never leave your couch facing away from your TV because you were unwilling to ask a friend for help. In your spiritual life, you must also get help – from God and other Christians.

Life isn't meant to be lived in solitude. We need to rely on our relationships with Jesus and others to encourage us to walk boldly, proclaim the power of God, show love, and apply discipline to our personal lives.

Week 1 – Day 5 Applied

Upward – Focus on God
What does today's passage tell you about God's character, promises, plans, or heart?

What attitude or emotion should that spark in you?

Inward – Personal Application
What does this passage reveal about your habits, attitude, and heart?

Is there an attitude you need to change, action you need to take, or sin you need to turn from?

Outward – Live It Out
What is the next step you must take to live out the truth of today's passage?

When and how will you take that step?

Week 1 – Day 6

Luke 5:16 – "But Jesus often withdrew to lonely places and prayed."

Some people enjoy alone time and seek it out. Others try to avoid it. But if we are going to follow Jesus, alone time is important.

Jesus often sought out alone time. And though he was physically alone and away from other people, He wasn't really alone. He prayed.

As a follower of Jesus, you should seek out alone time each day to pray. Jesus, being fully God and fully human, took time out of His daily schedule to pray. That ensured that His passions were burning brightly for heavenly things.

If Jesus withdrew to lonely places, prayed to God, and connected with His Heavenly Father, we must do the same.

Prayer is a time for confessing your sin to God, sharing your burdens with Him, and praising Him. It is also a time for listening to God.

It may seem like what I'm suggesting is too simple. Often, people seek out complicated processes to solve their problems. Instead, I propose that you take your spiritual walk back to the basics. Emphasize prayer this week. See if doing that helps you recognize what is extinguishing your spiritual fire.

Week 1 – Day 6 Applied

Upward – Focus on God
What does today's passage tell you about God's character, promises, plans, or heart?

What attitude or emotion should that spark in you?

Inward – Personal Application
What does this passage reveal about your habits, attitude, and heart?

Is there an attitude you need to change, action you need to take, or sin you need to turn from?

Outward – Live It Out
What is the next step you must take to live out the truth of today's passage?

When and how will you take that step?

WEEK 2

WHO IS STOKING MY PASSION FOR JESUS?

Week 2 – Day 1

Who Is Stoking My Passion for Jesus?

I'm sure that you have a favorite season of the year. Winter brings snowy days. Spring marks the return of warmth. And summer brings fun in the sun. But for me, fall reigns supreme as the greatest season of the year. My answer may be skewed by the fact that pie is my favorite dessert, and Thanksgiving happens to be in the fall. Besides pie, the fall season brings camping, college football, and cooler weather. This is the perfect time of year for me.

I love when the temperature finally dips down low enough to build a fire in my fireplace. If sitting by a fireplace brought in money, I would be set for life.

This year, as summer slipped into fall, we got to use the fireplace in our new house for the first time. My kids, Tripp and Brooke, are typical preschool kids – wildly adventurous and curious about life. They were eager to help me build the fire, so I decided it was time to teach them how. The steps are easy. I taught them how to check the damper, bring in logs from the woodshed, stack the logs, and light the fire. The fire started roaring as we settled down on the couch to watch some TV.

Every hour or so, I would get off the couch and walk to the fire. I would take my fire poker in my hand and open the metal screen that keeps the logs from falling on my living room floor. Logs do not burn evenly, which means that I have to move the half-burned logs onto the hotter coals and add more logs to the fire to keep it going.

Three hours after the fire started, I had made three trips to the fireplace to stoke the fire. Tripp looked up and asked me, "Dad, why do you have to move the burned logs to the middle and add new wood to the fire?"

My response was simple. I said, "Fires go out when they are left alone."

Fires can't burn alone. Wildfires are spurred on by high winds and dry climates. Campfires are stoked by campers adding branches. If a fire is left alone – without someone or something feeding the flames – the fire will eventually burn out. Wildfires, no matter how large, will burn out when the winds die down. Fires go out when they are left alone.

Your passion for Jesus is the same. Your passion will start to fade if your spiritual fire is left unattended. It is easy to think that your spiritual journey is solely dependent on your efforts. After all, you are the one reading your Bible, praying, worshipping, and drawing near to Jesus. But your spiritual fire will go out if you are the only one tending to it. You need other people investing in your spiritual growth. Your passion for Jesus is stoked when others are checking on your spiritual fire.

We Need Help Carrying Heavy Things

You need others to encourage and equip you to walk closer to Jesus. We call this discipleship. Every Jesus-follower needs other Jesus-followers to help stoke their passion for Jesus. We all need help carrying heavy things. This applies to everything in life. In the same way that you need help carrying a couch into your new house, you need help carrying stress, decisions, and discouragements.

Some situations will be *too big* for you to deal with on your own. You need comfort from others when facing the death of a loved one, loss of a job, or how to navigate a broken friendship.

Some situations will be *too confusing* for you to figure out on your own. Decisions about college majors, marriage, and which job to accept are life-changing and easier when you seek the advice of others.

Some situations will be *too stressful* for you to endure on your own. When options seem non-existent, you need encouragement to keep walking in the right direction.

There is a lie that is crippling students and young adults. Our culture tells us that maturity means living in isolation so that you can be the sole decision maker in your life. This lie tells you that the older you get, the less advice you need. It's common to hear a high school student say, "I can't wait until I'm eighteen years old. Then I'll do what I want." This may seem pure and noble, but there is a huge flaw with this. No one lies to you more than you do. Each day you convince yourself to make dumb decisions: procrastinating, dating a guy with questionable character, or rationalizing sin, to name a few. We can't trust ourselves! Our selfish desires skew reality and lead us to make poor decisions.

A mark of maturity isn't isolation but collaboration. A community of friends and mentors is essential for you to grow spiritually. The old adage is true – the people you surround yourself with are who you will become. *If you surround yourself with no one, you will quickly become a nobody.*

There will be times that you are tired, isolated, and spiritually weak. In those times, you will need encouragement and correction from others.

Hebrews 10:24-25 says, "And let us consider how we may spur one another on toward love and good deeds, not giving up meeting together, as some are in the habit of doing, but encouraging one another—and all the more as you see the Day approaching."

The worst decisions I have made in my life happened when I was tired, spiritually weak, or isolated.

Stoking your fire cannot be done on your own. Your passion will burn out if you do not live in community with other Jesus-followers. Jesus often ministers to us through other Christians. Disconnecting yourself from other Christians will cause your fire for Jesus to slowly fade. Besides, you never know when you will face a heavy situation. Everyone needs help carrying heavy things.

Unforeseen Dangers

One Friday afternoon, my coworker Chad and I were traveling back from an FCA camp discussing life and ministry. We were about a mile away from the church when Chad stopped his truck at a stop sign by a local school. Before we took our left turn, a teenage guy ran in front of Chad's truck. We were stopped, and the teenager could safely cross. It was obvious the young guy was exercising. We didn't think much about it and continued our conversation.

As the teenager ran by Chad's truck we noticed something alarming. Two large dogs were running at him. The dogs were on the opposite side of the busy street. I looked at Chad and said, "There is no way that these dogs are going to get across to this kid. He should be safe." Wouldn't you know, as soon as I ended the sentence, both vicious-looking dogs ran into oncoming traffic, growling and barking at the teenager.

The guy started to panic as he realized he couldn't get away from the dogs. There were no trees. There were no buildings. There were no fences to jump. Nothing was standing between this kid and two large dogs.

Chad quickly rolled down his window and yelled, "Hop in the back of my truck!" Like an Olympic sprinter, the teenager darted toward us. He made an ungraceful but successful jump into the bed of Chad's truck. The dogs barked for a few minutes but soon lost interest. Once it was safe, the teenager hopped out of Chad's truck and continued his jog.

Most of us think that we will be able to handle heavy situations and avoid sin before it gets us. We are confident we will be able to dodge a bad situation at just the right time, thank those who helped us, and continue on our way. Naively, we believe that we will be able to see the dangers that are coming our way.

This plan would be flawless if humans could predict the future. Unfortunately, we rarely know what situations we will encounter in our lives. Failing to build strong friendships with other Christians will leave you alone when heavy situations come. When we are faced with unexpected temptation or heavy situations, there's no guarantee that someone will arrive at the exact right moment with an escape route.

We need a community of people around us to help stoke our spiritual fires. Biblical friendships are essential for spiritual growth.

More than an Accountability Partner

Growing up in the early 2000s, several of my youth pastors told me that I needed an accountability partner. That sounded great and all, but I had no idea what an accountability partner was or what they were supposed to do. It was explained that you pick a person you regard as spiritually mature, and you meet together a few times a month to confess all your sins. You weren't supposed to pick a friend. Instead, you should choose someone spiritual who can ask you hard questions.

Someone may have explained it differently to you, but this is how the concept of accountability partners was conveyed to me.

That didn't settle well with me.

I thought the whole idea was a little awkward. I didn't want to have an extra person in my life who wasn't my friend but got access to my life. I didn't need a fake friend. I needed true friendships. Choosing an accountability partner felt like I was settling in my friendships. Only discussing spiritual things with an accountability partner outside my inner circle made me feel like I was missing the point somehow.

Accountability, the way I understood it at the time, didn't promise to give me support to grow spiritually. All it promised was awkwardness.

But I knew I needed people to help me establish guardrails in my life. The Old and New Testaments talk about establishing guardrails and seeking after wisdom. The prophets preached repentance and guidance. Proverbs instructs us to walk in wisdom. Paul reminds us in the Book of Ephesians to walk as those who are wise.

So, if establishing accountability with a specific accountability partner wasn't helpful, I needed to find out what would be.

Build Biblical Friendships

When I moved to college, I realized I could have natural accountability within biblical friendships. You need real friends. You do not need yes men who will not question your dumb decisions. You do not need hype people who only exist to make you happy. You need Gospel-centered friendships with people who are growing in their faith.

True friends are better than accountability partners. True friends will help you grow spiritually. True friends will ask you hard questions. True friends will encourage you to take steps of faith.

Young adults make the mistake of surrounding themselves with hundreds of shallow friendships. In the process, they fail to develop a few deep friendships. There isn't anything wrong with having plenty of friends. Problems arise when you don't have a few key friendships that are strong enough to weather difficult conversations.

Accountability within biblical friendships is simply more effective than forced accountability between acquaintances. The motivation of biblical friendship is to see both people grow in Jesus. The shared time and interests of a true friendship make real accountability possible.

Proverbs repeatedly teaches about the benefits of quality friendships. And Proverbs Chapter 27 is a gold mine of wisdom about friendships.

- **Proverbs 27:5-6** "Better is open rebuke than hidden love. Wounds from a friend can be trusted, but an enemy multiplies kisses."
- **Proverbs 27:9** "Perfume and incense bring joy to the heart, and the pleasantness of a friend springs from their heartfelt advice."
- **Proverbs 27:17** "As iron sharpens iron, so one person sharpens another."

Gospel-centered friendships will serve as a guardrail in your life in ways an accountability partner can't. How? Your friends see you more than an accountability partner would. It is easy to lie during one monthly meeting. On the other hand, you can't hide your behaviors and struggles from close friends. The closer the proximity, the greater potential for accountability and discipleship to occur. We all need people who can speak into our lives on a day-to-day basis. Those true friendships will shape our lives more than an accountability partner ever could.

Creating Gospel-Centered Friendships

There isn't a foolproof guide to developing lifelong friendships with Jesus-followers. Life is too messy for such a guide to exist. Everyone's situation is unique. But there are some universal principles that will help you create Gospel-centered friendships. Here are a few:

Strong friendships are built on trust, proximity, and common beliefs. You can't talk to a person once a month and expect to be close friends. Friendships become stronger as you spend time together. As you add responsibilities, jobs, and family members, you can forget to include other people in your life. Start looking for ways to invite friends into the activities you are already doing (eating meals, watching sporting events, weekly small groups, and so on).

Begin having deeper conversations with your friends. You will notice if they are open to talking about real issues and struggles or if they shy away from deep conversations. By all means, slowly walk into deeper conversations – you don't have to air all your laundry and beliefs at once. But be intentional to bring up faith topics. Start by getting involved in a small group in your local church and see what friendships develop from there.

Realize not all friendships will be deep friendships. Some have a hard time with this truth. It is OK to have surface-level friendships. That is the world we live in. Certain coworkers will never become deep friends. Don't stress about that. The key is to have a few deep friendships in the midst of the various acquaintances you have.

Obviously, this list isn't exhaustive. The older we get the worse we are at making friends. Remember the elementary school version of you? Most of us were comfortable enough to walk up to another kid and ask them if they wanted to be friends. We weren't nervous about the prospect of meeting someone new.

Along the way we have been burned, backstabbed, and ignored more times than we can count. Messy relationships have caused us to avoid being transparent and honest with people for fear that they will one day use our vulnerability against us. We need to return to the elementary school days of seeing people as potential friends, not potential backstabbers.

Who Is Stoking Your Passion for Jesus?

In Matthew 13, a large crowd gathered around Jesus by the lake. So He went out on a boat a short distance from the shore and began to teach them using parables – short stories with spiritual lessons.

Matthew 13:3-9 tells us, "Then he told them many things in parables, saying: 'A farmer went out to sow his seed. As he was scattering the seed, some fell along the path, and the birds came and ate it up. Some fell on rocky places, where it did not have much soil. It sprang up quickly, because the soil was shallow. But when the sun came up, the plants were scorched, and they withered because they had no root. Other seed fell among thorns, which grew up and choked the plants. Still other seed fell on good soil, where it produced a crop—a hundred, sixty or thirty times what was sown. Whoever has ears, let them hear.'"

I doubt you are a farmer, so this parable may seem a bit strange to you. At its core, the parable discusses the different responses people have when they encounter Jesus. In the story we see that one soil produces no crops, one soil produces some crops, and one soil produces ample crops. Jesus uses this imagery to describe how people respond to the good news of Jesus' love and mercy. Some grow spiritually, others show interest in Jesus, and others don't have any connection to Jesus.

I used to read this parable like I was the only person making the decision about how I respond to the good news of Jesus. But it's apparent that Jesus isn't talking about individuals as much as he is talking about how groups of people respond. If we spend all our time with people who are hardened to faith in Jesus, we will become dry like them.

What type of soil are your friends? Are they hardened to the things of Jesus? Do they lack deep roots and are burned when hard times come? Or, are they growing in their faith? Where you are planted determines how deep your roots grow.

We need real friendships with people who are deeply rooted in Jesus. Do you have to cut off all your non-Christian friends? Maybe, maybe not. That depends on if they cause you to fall into sin. Christians shouldn't withdraw from non-Christians. That makes it impossible to fulfill the Great Commission in Matthew 28:18-20. It does mean, however, that our closest friendships need to be with people who are passionately following Jesus. They are the good soil. They are the ones who will help us stoke our passions for Jesus when heavy situations come our way.

The bottom line is that friendships don't magically develop. Having Gospel-centered friendships takes intentionality and transparency. Those can be hard, but the end result is worth it.

So, who is stoking your passion for Jesus? Remember, fires burn out when they are left alone.

Now What?

Passage to Study: Proverbs 27

Questions:
1. What type of soil are your closest friends?
2. Why is it difficult to have spiritual conversations with your friends?
3. What spiritual conversations do you need to have with your friends this week?

Week 2 – Day 2

2 Timothy 1:6 – "For this reason I remind you to fan into flame the gift of God, which is in you through the laying on of my hands."

In these verses, the Apostle Paul encouraged Timothy, a young pastor in the early church. Timothy's fire for Jesus wasn't burning out. Paul was encouraging Timothy to grow closer to Jesus and use his gifts like never before. "Fan the flame" is a present-tense verb that means to keep on fanning the flame. Paul is saying, "Stoke your fire for Jesus daily, and it will burn like never before!"

This is a truth we need to remember – we can stoke our fire for Jesus before it burns out. Even if your spiritual life is great, your passion for Jesus can burn brighter and hotter than it is right now!

The Spirit of God was working through Timothy, and Paul encouraged him to keep stoking the fire God had placed inside of him. In his two letters to Timothy, Paul instructed Timothy on how to interact with others, lead a church, and stoke his spiritual fire for Jesus. Even as a successful pastor, Timothy had other people help him stoke his passion for Jesus.

Spiritual growth will not happen if you live in isolation. Each of us needs others to check on our spiritual fire and encourage us to fan the flame and grow closer to Jesus.

Week 2 – Day 2 Applied

Upward – Focus on God
What does today's passage tell you about God's character, promises, plans, or heart?

What attitude or emotion should that spark in you?

Inward – Personal Application
What does this passage reveal about your habits, attitude, and heart?

Is there an attitude you need to change, action you need to take, or sin you need to turn from?

Outward – Live It Out
What is the next step you must take to live out the truth of today's passage?

When and how will you take that step?

Week 2 – Day 3

Romans 12:15 – "Rejoice with those who rejoice; mourn with those who mourn."

This straightforward verse should be the baseline for how your biblical friendships operate. Real friends choose to share the highs and lows of their life with each other.

We typically think about community as sitting around a living room sharing one another's feelings. But being a Christian who has Christlike friends is more than that. Biblical friendships are rooted in the Gospel. These types of friendships point to Jesus and encourage us when life get tough.

Be happy when times are happy. How often do you hang out with other Christians? Contrary to popular belief, Christians can have fun! What activities do your friends enjoy? Watch ball games together. Have a weekly board game night. Meet for coffee once a month. Have spiritual conversations along the way.

Be sad when times are sad. There is more to friendship than enjoying the high points in life. True friendships reveal themselves during the hard times. Biblical friendships are an encouraging presence as you face difficult times.

Week 2 – Day 3 Applied

Upward – Focus on God
What does today's passage tell you about God's character, promises, plans, or heart?

What attitude or emotion should that spark in you?

Inward – Personal Application
What does this passage reveal about your habits, attitude, and heart?

Is there an attitude you need to change, action you need to take, or sin you need to turn from?

Outward – Live It Out
What is the next step you must take to live out the truth of today's passage?

When and how will you take that step?

Week 2 – Day 4

Proverbs 15:22 – "Plans fail for lack of counsel, but with many advisers they succeed."

In your life, do you forge ahead with your plans, confident in your own personal navigation skills? Or do you seek out the opinions of others as you make decisions?

We have all been there – convinced we are making the right decisions only to find out our plan wasn't as solid as we had hoped.

Why does this happen? Why does it seem like we are consistently choosing the wrong path or making the wrong decisions? It is because everyone has gaps or blind spots – areas we can't see or fully understand. Gaps can come from any number of sources, but they keep us from seeing a big-picture view of our situation.

Reducing the gaps in your judgement and decision making starts by having close friends who will give you biblical advice. Great decisions are made when we listen to godly wisdom from those closest to us.

We must invite others to help us make decisions, especially those that could impact our spiritual life.

Week 2 – Day 4 Applied

Upward – Focus on God
What does today's passage tell you about God's character, promises, plans, or heart?

What attitude or emotion should that spark in you?

Inward – Personal Application
What does this passage reveal about your habits, attitude, and heart?

Is there an attitude you need to change, action you need to take, or sin you need to turn from?

Outward – Live It Out
What is the next step you must take to live out the truth of today's passage?

When and how will you take that step?

Week 2 – Day 5

Proverbs 20:5 – "The purposes of a person's heart are deep waters, but one who has insight draws them out."

Others have a way of helping us see our potential and affirming our skills.

Those closest to us can see what we are capable of becoming and how God is moving in our lives. Close friendships and mentors can be a positive force for fanning the flame God has placed inside of us. Others notice ways God has gifted you and ways He is at work in your life that you won't see.

Identifying your potential is the first part. Godly mentors will give you the confidence you need to start reaching your God-given potential to bring others closer to Jesus.

Affirming your skills is the next part. Godly friends will point out where they see God at work in your life. They will also give you the encouragement you need to keep serving God even if it's hard or inconvenient.

Week 2 – Day 5 Applied

Upward – Focus on God
What does today's passage tell you about God's character, promises, plans, or heart?

What attitude or emotion should that spark in you?

Inward – Personal Application
What does this passage reveal about your habits, attitude, and heart?

Is there an attitude you need to change, action you need to take, or sin you need to turn from?

Outward – Live It Out
What is the next step you must take to live out the truth of today's passage?

When and how will you take that step?

Week 2 – Day 6

Proverbs 27:17 – "As iron sharpens iron, so one person sharpens another."

Is your spiritual passion dull? You might be hanging out with spiritually dull people. Spiritually dull people are those who are stagnant in their faith or are altogether not following Jesus. Metals are sharpened by stronger metals, not weaker ones.

Spiritual conversations between friends will sharpen our relationship with Jesus. These conversations cause us to wrestle with tough spiritual questions and help us apply God's truth to our lives. We become dull from the wear and tear of our lives. The best way for us to sharpen our spiritual lives is to have spiritual conversations about God's Word with close friends.

Here are a few ways friends will sharpen your faith:

They pray for and with you.
They keep you accountable.
They influence you to make godly decisions.
They inspire you to serve in areas of your giftedness.
They encourage you to read and apply God's Word.

Who are two or three people who are stoking your fire for Jesus?

Week 2 – Day 6 Applied

Upward – Focus on God
What does today's passage tell you about God's character, promises, plans, or heart?

What attitude or emotion should that spark in you?

Inward – Personal Application
What does this passage reveal about your habits, attitude, and heart?

Is there an attitude you need to change, action you need to take, or sin you need to turn from?

Outward – Live It Out
What is the next step you must take to live out the truth of today's passage?

When and how will you take that step?

WEEK 3

WHAT IS GOD TEACHING ME THROUGH HIS WORD?

Week 3 – Day 1

What Is God Teaching Me through His Word?

If I write a children's book, I already have the perfect title for it. The book will be called *I Hate Bees.* To be fair, I don't hate all bees. I only hate yellow jackets. I know, I know, "hate" is a strong word. Well, yellow jackets caused me to catch myself on fire. Let me rephrase in case you missed that. Yellow jackets forced me to stop, drop, and roll to extinguish actual flames from my body.

A few years after Anne and I got married, we moved to a Christian camp in the foothills of the Great Smoky Mountains National Park in East Tennessee. Part of my job there included helping a few other guys maintain more than 350 acres of land at the camp. Many days were spent mowing, cleaning fields, and doing general maintenance to the buildings and grounds.

One summer afternoon I was trimming tall grass around the creeks on the property. That chore wasn't too bad. The only issues you would run into were copperhead snakes and yellow jackets. We were used to the wildlife around the camp and were careful while we worked, so it was usually fine. I was working alone on this particular afternoon, and I drove a flatbed truck around with plenty of weed eater string, gasoline, and kerosene. The kerosene was for the slim chance I ran into a yellow jacket nest that was close to one of our primary buildings.

I was working around the creek behind my house, minding my own business, when I felt a bee sting me in the neck. Bees in East Tennessee don't play around. They go straight for the kill shot. Once I realized I was stung, it was too late. The second, third, and fourth bees stung as quickly as the first did. The only defense I had was to throw the weed eater down and run like a maniac away from the bees. I looked like a fool.

The bees needed a few minutes to settle down. After all, I did attack their home with a power tool. Once they stopped swarming, I walked over to assess the situation. The nest was on the edge of the creek. I wasn't cool with having thousands of bees living where my son played. I walked to the truck, grabbed the five gallon can of kerosene, poured it on the bees' nest, and lit the fuel. Flames engulfed the yellow jackets, and I walked down the creek to continue trimming the tall grass.

One hour later I ran out of fuel in my weed eater. I walked back to the truck and noticed that bees were still flying out of the nest. By this time the flames had burned out and the bees were back in full force protecting their home. I really needed to get rid of the bees so they didn't hurt my family. I grabbed the kerosene from the truck and walked over to the bees. There was a small flame visible on the charred bees' nest, so I dowsed it in kerosene and went back to work.

Another hour passed, and I was out of gas in the weed eater again. I walked back to the truck and couldn't believe my eyes – the bees were still alive and active at the nest! What kind of animal can survive two rounds of fire? Frustrated, I walked over to the truck and once again grabbed the kerosene. I noticed a problem when I picked the can up. There wasn't any more kerosene in the five gallon can. I had used all of it on my first two fiery attacks on the bees.

What I did next was not the brightest moment in my life. I promise that I'm a smart guy, but this moment had to be one of the dumbest in my life.

Out of kerosene, I turned to the five gallon can of gasoline that was sitting next to it on the truck. Fueled by frustration at the bees and exhaustion from the summer heat, I decided to throw gasoline on the yellow jacket nest.

Like I said, I'm a smart guy. I came up with a plan to throw gasoline on the nest and lead a line of gasoline far enough away so I wouldn't blow up. This is how people blow things up in the movies, so it had to work.

The plan depended on one thing – there couldn't be any flames on the nest that would ignite the gasoline before I was ready. I did a quick check for flames and didn't see anything. It was time to soak the yellow jackets with gasoline and light this fire from a safe distance.

I stood close to the bees' nest with the can of gasoline in my hands. With both hands I began to pour gasoline on the nest. All was going according to plan for the first five seconds. Then, the worst-case scenario happened. A flame began following the stream of gasoline up to the five gallon can I was holding. Before I could throw the can, the flames reached the can and it exploded in my hands. Fire, gasoline, and angry bees were everywhere. I was fully engulfed in flames.

(As an aside, I only attended one day of Boy Scouts when I was a kid. During this session they taught us two life lessons: First, hug a tree if you are lost in the woods.

Second, stop, drop, and roll if you catch yourself on fire. At the time, I was in elementary school. I didn't know that I would use both of these techniques before I was twenty-five years old.)

Back to the story. Here I am, on fire and running through a field like Ricky Bobby, when I remembered what I learned twenty years before in Boy Scouts. Stop. Drop. Roll. In an instant, I fell to the ground and started rolling. I was able to extinguish the flames from my clothing. Luckily, I walked away with a few non-severe burns, destroyed clothes, and charred eyebrows.

I walked back to my house a bit shaken by the flames and tried to think about how I was going to explain this to my wife. As I opened the door Anne looked at me and asked, "Why do I smell burning human hair?" I informed her that her intelligent husband lost a battle against yellow jackets. Fearing that she didn't believe me, I brought Anne out to see the fire by the creek. But by the time I put new clothes on and we walked to our backyard the flames were almost gone. Only angry bees and a large burned circle remained on the ground.

Sustainable Fires

That was the hottest and brightest fire I have ever seen. But its large flames died out in less than fifteen minutes because it was only fueled by gasoline. Gasoline is great at starting a fire, but it won't cause a fire to last.

Some of us run into the same issue in our spiritual walk with Jesus. We see our passion for Jesus burn large and bright, but when we return to our normal routines, the fire burns out because we fail to fan the flames. Sure, the quick blaze of passion for Jesus is large, impressive, and even caused other people to step back in amazement.

But our experience at an event, camp, or retreat didn't change our daily habits once we returned home. Camps are great at igniting your passion for Jesus, but spiritual disciplines are what continue to fuel that passion.

If you don't fuel your passion for Jesus with God's Word, you will find that your passion slowly burns out. Remember, a fire needs fuel, oxygen, and a spark to exist. Your spiritual growth needs to be fueled each day as you train yourself in godliness (1 Timothy 4:7-8).

If you have ever built a fire you know that there are some fuels that are better than others. There are some things that you can burn and some things that you can't burn! Some items will burn bright and hot, but burn out quickly (like gasoline). Other items will burn slow and long – this is ideal for building a sustainable fire.

Every seasoned camper knows that building a fire that solely consists of dried leaves is a waste of time and a waste of a match. Leaves will burn, but they aren't efficient as the primary source of the fire. Wood is a far better fuel for your fire. It burns slowly and creates coals that will continue to heat the fire throughout the night. You need plenty of small sticks, logs, and branches to build a fire.

But a fire won't burn forever on one log.

Daily Discipline of Stoking Your Fire

Fires need to be fed for them to continue. It's really a pretty simple system. A fire needs logs added to it every so often for the fire to continue to burn brightly and produce heat. If you are camping and want to wake up to a warm fire, you must wake up several times in the night to add a log or two to the fire. If not, the fire will go out.

Many people feel spiritually cold and powerless because they have failed to stoke their spiritual passion. The best way to stoke your spiritual fire is to study, memorize, and apply the Bible.

The Bible is the fuel for our souls. Much like your stomach longs for nutrients, your soul craves the spiritual nourishment that comes from God's Word. Your passion for Jesus is fueled by your intake of God's Word.

You can't eat once a week and expect your body to grow correctly. Your spiritual growth works in the same way. You need to daily feed on the Bible to fuel your passion for Jesus. It is like throwing another log on the fire. It stokes your passion for Jesus.

Similarly, you can't eat junk food every day and expect your body to grow correctly. Your spiritual growth works in the same way. If your time is spent taking in anything and everything *except* God's Word, it's like eating junk food all the time. But if you commit to studying and learning from the Word of God, it's like eating healthy food all the time.

A great example of this concept playing out in our lives is coming home from a church camp or weekend retreat. Most people feel closer to God while at a camp or retreat than when they come home. The main reason for this is that while you were away you were deeply studying God's Word. You sang songs with Bible verses in them. You heard a pastor explain the Bible. You were in small groups that discussed the Bible. And you were personally exploring the Bible during your devotion time. You were taking in the Bible every time you turned around!

Then you went home.
You entered back into your routines and habits.
You slowly lost focus on God's Word.
Your time was filled with other activities.
And your passion for Jesus started to fade.

That happens because you weren't fueling your soul with God's Word – you were feeding your spirit junk.

Jesus said this about food, fuel, life, and the words of God in Matthew 4:4: "... It is written, 'Man shall not live by bread alone, but by every word that comes from the mouth of God.'"

Satan was tempting Jesus in this passage of Scripture. After forty days of fasting from food, Satan tried to get Jesus to fill His stomach.

Jesus' response was that the stomach only gives us a physical life, not spiritual life. True life and passion for God is fueled by consuming God's words because the Bible divinely penetrates our lives and shows us more about the Savior who laid down His life for us.

What Is God Teaching Me through His Word?

We have plenty of excuses for not reading the Bible. We are too busy, the words are too big and hard to understand, we are confused by the stories, or the Bible seems boring. But Jesus takes obedience seriously. In John 15:14 He said, "You are my friends if you do what I command." Can we say that we love Jesus if we blatantly ignore Jesus' commands? Many attempt to. They haven't taken time to read the Bible, discover who Jesus is, and be encouraged by His words. They attempt to live good moral lives apart from reading the Bible and never experience the life Jesus desires for them.

Dwight L. Moody said, "The Bible will keep you from sin, or sin will keep you from the Bible." This truth perfectly describes the tension that exists. Either you read God's Word, stoke your spiritual fire, and submit to Jesus' leadership (trying to avoid sin), or you avoid God's Word, experience spiritual burnout, and submit to your own leadership (more easily falling into sin).

How has your study of God's Word been going? Are you attending a local church and learning more about Jesus through group study? Are you daily feeding on the Scriptures as your source of life and wisdom? Have you built biblical friendships that spur you to find wisdom in the Bible?

If you have no idea, you can ask yourself this simple question: "What is God teaching me through His Word?" If you can't come up with an answer, it might be that you haven't been reading your Bible or you haven't been reading it carefully.

The goal of Bible study isn't to get a check on a checklist. It isn't about posting an awesome picture of your devotion on Instagram. The purpose of Bible study is for you to learn from and experience Jesus. This can't be done if you rush through your study or rarely pick up your Bible. There are plenty of ways to read the Bible. You can do character studies, word studies, or theme studies. You can read book-by-book or chronologically. It is important that you develop this daily discipline. Why? Because without a daily discipline of Bible intake, your passion for Jesus will slowly burn out.

Think about the time you felt most on fire for Jesus. How often did you read your Bible that week? How many spiritual conversations did you have with adults and friends? How many times did you worship Jesus? I'm sure the answer to these questions is a ton! Camps pull you away from your normal schedule and habits and refocus your attention on Jesus. But a weekend event, weekly worship service, or summer camp can't fuel your spiritual growth for an entire year.

When you come back from an event, you won't be able to keep the camp pace up. But worship, service, spiritual conversations, groups, and Bible study must continue when you get home. If not, your passion for Jesus will slowly burn out.

We need to build in a daily habit of learning from God's Word. It encourages, corrects, teaches, and equips us to live for Christ in our daily lives.

Now What?

Passage to Study: Psalm 119:89-112

Questions:

1. How would you rate your daily discipline of Bible study? (10 being incredible and 1 being non-existent.) Why would you choose that number?
2. What excuses do you use for not reading your Bible? What are some ways you can overcome your excuses and make time for reading Scripture?

Week 3 – Day 2

2 Timothy 3:16-17 – "All Scripture is God-breathed and is useful for teaching, rebuking, correcting and training in righteousness, so that the servant of God may be thoroughly equipped for every good work."

How do you use God's Word? Is the Bible your go-to for encouragement and inspiration? Do you dive deep into each verse to learn the Biblical truths present? Does the Bible spark your worship for Jesus as you read about His redemptive mission?

All of the Bible is from God and is useful in a variety of ways. Paul tells us that the Bible is useful for teaching, rebuking, correcting, and training.

Teaching: Sound doctrine (what you believe about God) is essential for every Christian.

Rebuking: The Bible shows us our failures, mistakes, and sins. Why would it do this? Because it also brings the hope and assurance of Jesus.

Correction: Like the loving Father that He is, God gives us the Bible to correct us with grace, truth, and mercy so that we will mature in our faith.

Training: Some view training as a negative process, but training is the only way to stretch our muscles and grow. The Bible stretches our views and practices of love, hope, encouragement, and service. It trains us to live more like Jesus.

Week 3 – Day 2 Applied

Upward – Focus on God
What does today's passage tell you about God's character, promises, plans, or heart?

What attitude or emotion should that spark in you?

Inward – Personal Application
What does this passage reveal about your habits, attitude, and heart?

Is there an attitude you need to change, action you need to take, or sin you need to turn from?

Outward – Live It Out
What is the next step you must take to live out the truth of today's passage?

When and how will you take that step?

Week 3 – Day 3

Hebrews 4:12 – "For the word of God is alive and active. Sharper than any double-edged sword, it penetrates even to dividing soul and spirit, joints and marrow; it judges the thoughts and attitudes of the heart."

Have you heard the expression "just the tip of the iceberg"? People use the phrase to describe a situation that has more going on beneath the surface. Everyone has deeper motivations than outsiders see.

You can't hide issues from God. He sees the true you. He knows your motivations. His Word can reach the deepest areas of your life and transform you from the inside. Growing in Jesus isn't about acting the right way or saying the correct words. It is about true life and heart change. That happens as the Word of God begins to work in your life, shaping you into the likeness of Jesus.

Our actions may fool others, but God knows our intentions. As we read the Bible His words not only change our actions, the Spirit of God moves in the core of who we are and changes our motivations.

Week 3 – Day 3 Applied

Upward – Focus on God
What does today's passage tell you about God's character, promises, plans, or heart?

What attitude or emotion should that spark in you?

Inward – Personal Application
What does this passage reveal about your habits, attitude, and heart?

Is there an attitude you need to change, action you need to take, or sin you need to turn from?

Outward – Live It Out
What is the next step you must take to live out the truth of today's passage?

When and how will you take that step?

Week 3 – Day 4

Joshua 1:8 – "Keep this Book of the Law always on your lips; meditate on it day and night, so that you may be careful to do everything written in it. Then you will be prosperous and successful."

Campers know the importance of making a fire. When you are miles from electricity, a fire provides warmth, a place to cook, light, and a deterrent for animals. I like to gather two or three times as much firewood as I think I will need to get through the night. Every thirty minutes to an hour the fire will need another log or two. If we all fall asleep and no one puts a log on the fire, it will be completely burned out by the morning.

The book of Joshua begins with Joshua leading God's people after Moses died. The people of Israel wandered in the wilderness for forty years because of their lack of faith. Now, the next generation was positioned to enter the Promised Land. God commissioned Joshua to hold firm to the Book of the Law before he led the people into a foreign land filled with ungodly cultures.

God encouraged Joshua to keep the Law on his lips – to read it, to talk about it, and to obey it. When negative influences and potential spiritual fire extinguishers surrounded Joshua, God's said to meditate on His Word. Careful obedience to God's Word means that we must surround ourselves with God's truth throughout our day. Reading God's Word isn't enough. There is an expectation for us to read the Bible, understand what it says, and apply it to our lives. Then, in the same way God told Joshua, we will be prosperous.

Week 3 – Day 4 Applied

Upward – Focus on God
What does today's passage tell you about God's character, promises, plans, or heart?

What attitude or emotion should that spark in you?

Inward – Personal Application
What does this passage reveal about your habits, attitude, and heart?

Is there an attitude you need to change, action you need to take, or sin you need to turn from?

Outward – Live It Out
What is the next step you must take to live out the truth of today's passage?

When and how will you take that step?

Week 3 – Day 5

Psalm 119:9 – "How can a young person stay on the path of purity? By living according to your word."

What does it take to gain wisdom? One view that is prevalent in our culture is that wisdom comes only through personal experience. The only way to be wise, some would say, is to make lots of mistakes. How else will you learn right from wrong?

Firsthand experience isn't the only way to gain wisdom and sound judgement. We gain wisdom by reading, asking questions, observing others' good and bad decisions, and reading the Bible.

The Bible isn't a book full of rules and regulations. Sure, it contains rules and commandments for us to follow, but the Bible is more than a legal document. Have you noticed that the Bible includes accounts of people failing miserably? In fact, some of the accounts were written by the people who failed! Most of us wouldn't want to record our failures, but the Bible shows us examples of when people obeyed *and* disobeyed God. It shows us that we can make wise decisions. The Bible gives us a source of wisdom to help us limit dumb mistakes when we are young. As we live according to God's Word, our passion for Jesus will burn brighter than our passion for other things.

Thinking leads to action. The best way for us to pursue purity is to live according to God's Word. We must take it in daily and apply its teachings.

Week 3 – Day 5 Applied

Upward – Focus on God
What does today's passage tell you about God's character, promises, plans, or heart?

What attitude or emotion should that spark in you?

Inward – Personal Application
What does this passage reveal about your habits, attitude, and heart?

Is there an attitude you need to change, action you need to take, or sin you need to turn from?

Outward – Live It Out
What is the next step you must take to live out the truth of today's passage?

When and how will you take that step?

Week 3 – Day 6

James 1:22 – "Do not merely listen to the word, and so deceive yourselves. Do what it says."

How many times have you read the Bible and couldn't remember what you read fifteen minutes later?

It happens to all of us, doesn't it? We attend worship services and camps and read our Bibles, but we never seem to put God's Word into action in our lives.

The Bible speaks about reading, meditating on, and studying God's Word. The original audience would have understood that everything you study and read should be put into practice.

James started to see a shift in this understanding. The first century church was constantly attacked by false teachers. Many Christians would become confused about what they believed. Some stopped practicing their faith and were content with merely learning about God and not applying His teachings.

We experience this same temptation. We feel pressure to keep our faith intellectual, learning about Jesus without living out what He teaches. Your passion for Jesus can't burn brightly if you constantly hide the light. The Bible was meant to be read *and* applied. Jesus taught for transformation. Others should see what God is teaching you through the Bible because you are living those lessons out in your everyday life.

Week 3 – Day 6 Applied

Upward – Focus on God
What does today's passage tell you about God's character, promises, plans, or heart?

What attitude or emotion should that spark in you?

Inward – Personal Application
What does this passage reveal about your habits, attitude, and heart?

Is there an attitude you need to change, action you need to take, or sin you need to turn from?

Outward – Live It Out
What is the next step you must take to live out the truth of today's passage?

When and how will you take that step?

WEEK 4

WHAT IS CONSUMING MY THOUGHTS AND TIME?

Week 4 – Day 1

What Is Consuming My Thoughts and Time?

Snow days are the saving grace of the winter season. It might as well snow if it has to be cold outside!

There was one perfect snow storm when I was in middle school. It was one of those storms teenagers dream about. School was cancelled. Everyone woke up to find fresh powder that was perfect for sledding and tubing. Yes, I did say tubing. We would inflate ski tubes and push them down a snow-covered hill. Several of us could pack on one tube, and it traveled faster than a sled. It was a middle school guy's dream – speed and looming death.

During this particular snow I invited several friends over to my house to hang out. Our house was situated on a corner lot with a road that was perfect for snow tubing. The road had a steep grade for us to go fast down the hill. There was just one minor issue. The road ended with a huge ditch. We would go flying off the road and fall to our death if we didn't jump off the tube at the right time. My friends and I weren't worried about it at all though. Our parents stood at the bottom of the hill to catch the tube once we let go and fell off. The plan was foolproof – we would let go of the tube and roll off into the snow when we passed the last mailbox. It was time to ride!

This worked like a charm for hours! Each of my friends took turns riding the tube down the snowy hill. Everyone let go and fell into the snow in a fit of joy, and the parents caught the slow-moving tube as it reached the bottom of the hill. Round and round we went. Up the hill, down the hill. My friends and I were having a blast.

Except for Jesse.

Jesse was my friend's neighbor. I didn't hang out with him that often, but from what I gathered he was a fearful guy. He never took a turn on the tube and gave up his spot to let someone else ride down the hill. I kept passing him and asking if he wanted to jump on the tube, but he declined every time. I felt bad for the guy. He was missing an incredible experience!

I must have asked him one hundred times before he relented and decided to tube down the hill with us. He was finally ready to conquer his fears and tube down the snowy road.

Jesse, Robert, and I jumped on the tube to make the epic trip down the hill. Before we kicked off, we reminded Jesse of the only rule – let go and jump off at the last mailbox. He nodded, and the next thing we knew we were flying down the hill like a rocket.

Robert and I were yelling and high fiving each other while we were tubing down the road. Our adrenaline was pumping. Then I noticed Jesse didn't share our enthusiasm. He was terrified of the snow and speed. I didn't think much of his fear because there wasn't anything I could do. We were sailing down a snowy road on a rubber tube. Jesse would see. Nothing would go wrong.

Two minutes into our tubing we reached the last mailbox. To make sure Jesse remembered what to do, I yelled out for him to jump. And with that, Robert and I bailed off the tube and rolled to a safe stop in the snow. Once we reoriented from our controlled crash, we realized that Jesse didn't jump off the tube. In perfect unison, we looked each other in the eyes, then looked back at Jesse still holding onto the tube. He wasn't letting go. As he got closer to the parents they began yelling, "Jesse, let go! Let go of the tube! You are going to fly into the ditch! Please, let go!"

But Jesse didn't let go. Instead, he held onto the handles even tighter. He was clinging to the tube as if his life depended on it. Ironically, the thing he was clinging to was about to bring him a great deal of harm.

The parents braced for impact. The tube finally made it to the bottom of the road and the parents were the only barrier between Jesse and the deep, wooded ditch. Jesse had one last opportunity to let go and roll to safety, but he didn't. Jesse hit the row of parents like a giant bowling ball running over parent-sized bowling pins. The force of the collision caused Jesse to catapult about eight feet into the air and into the ditch. We all stood in frozen silence as if Jesse was moving in slow motion. Mother Nature even seemed to stop snowing in an effort to watch Jesse's flight through the frosty air.

Jesse landed with a loud crash. He emerged minutes later with a few scratches and a list of fears that had just been validated. He would be OK, but he would never tube in the snow again.

Unable to Let Go

This storyline has replayed several times throughout my life. No, I haven't been tubing with Jesse recently. The stakes have been higher and the situations more serious.

There have been times in my life when I decided to cling to something that would lead to pain and uncertainty. Even worse, I knew the potential dangers ahead but decided to jump on the idea. "I'll know when to stop," I told myself.

I have held on to plans that were self-centered.

I have held on to relationships that weren't God-honoring.

I have held on to hope that more possessions would bring more happiness.

And the lie that I believed was a simple one. I believed that I could just let go whenever I wanted. I would set boundaries and say, "I can stop whenever I want to" or "This doesn't have control over me." Or the worst: "I'm just having fun. This isn't going to harm me."

Then it would happen.

I would pass a point and realize that I was unable to let go on my own. I was clinging to the thing that would lead to pain and heartbreak. The sin and poor choices I believed I could control would eventually control me. Sometimes, I listened to the counsel of those around me and let go before I crashed. Other times, I found myself unable to let go and had to pay the price that comes with the road running out.

Every time I have been in these situations, I fully believed I was in control of my relationships, possessions, and plans. That belief blinded me to any dangers that were ahead of me. When we find ourselves clinging to a plan, person, or possession that isn't God-honoring, our spiritual fire isn't what it could be.

I don't know what it is for you. Unless I know you personally, I'll never know your specific situation. What I do know is that everyone has *something*. We all cling to things other than Jesus sometimes. And those things will suffocate our passion for Jesus. See, fire needs oxygen to survive. If you take away all the oxygen, the fire will burn out. On the flip side, the more wind you have, the larger a fire grows.

The same is true for stoking your fire for Jesus. If you cling to something that takes you away from God's plan, your passion for Him weakens. The more you allow the Spirit of God to work in your life, the hotter and brighter your fire will burn for Jesus.

When we quench the Spirit of God and begin to cling to other things, our passion for Jesus fades away like a suffocating fire.

Clinging to Sin vs. Clinging to God

Most of us would readily admit that sin stops us from stoking our spiritual passion for Jesus. Clinging to any situation that isn't God-honoring is not the best idea for someone who wants to grow in faith. So why do we do it?

Why do we cling to plans, people, and possessions that lead us away from our commitment to Jesus?

The answer is this: We place far too much faith in our ability to say no at just the right time, and we place far too little faith in God's plan for us.

The worst way for us to avoid sin is thinking, "I can let go of this whenever I want."

The best way for us to do it is to make sure our thoughts and time are centered on Jesus.

The Bible has much to say about what we spend our time thinking about and doing. Here are a few examples to get you started.

> *2 Corinthians 10:5*
> *We demolish arguments and every pretension that sets itself up against the knowledge of God, and we take captive every thought to make it obedient to Christ.*
>
> *Ephesians 5:15*
> *Be very careful, then, how you live–not as unwise but as wise– making the most of every opportunity.*

Philippians 4:8
Finally, brothers and sisters, whatever is true, whatever is noble, whatever is right, whatever is pure, whatever is lovely, whatever is admirable—if anything is excellent or praiseworthy—think about such things.

What is consuming your thoughts and time?

It might be that a show you watch has you preoccupied with themes that are counter to how God commands you to live. At the very least, the media you consume might keep you from something incredible – writing a book, preparing for a mission trip, or building biblical friendships.

It might be that the music you listen to while you take a run or do homework is filling your head with thoughts that don't honor God. You need to look at the lyrics of your favorite songs. You might be surprised at the references you missed or overlooked.

It might be that the conversations you engage in with your friends aren't uplifting. Constant jokes at the expense of others, angry and cruel topics, and endless complaining are going to pull your mind away from God, not closer.

Your brain is always working. Every second, it is processing information, remembering things, controlling functions in your body, obeying habits you've created, and so much more. All day long, there are things demanding your attention and mental energy. It is impossible to be completely in control of every single thing going on in your mind.

If you are trying to stoke your spiritual fire, you must monitor your thoughts and time as closely as you can. If you don't, it's like walking away from a campfire and being surprised by the results when you return hours later. It could go out completely while you aren't watching.

God tells us in His Word that our thoughts are important and that we must use our time wisely. If you want to stoke your spiritual passion for Jesus, you must take action on those truths.

What Is Consuming My Thoughts and Time?

If your passion for Jesus is burning out, I bet your passion for something else is burning hotter. We rarely enter seasons where we have no passion. We are always clinging to *something*.

Normally, we replace our passion for Jesus with a passion for something lesser. The flame for Jesus slowly burns out because something other than Jesus is consuming our thoughts and time.

What we think about, hope for, and spend our time on dictates the direction of our lives. When our eyes are set on Jesus, our steps will fall in line.

It is important for you to assess your current spiritual state. Consider what you spend your time thinking about, what your deepest hopes are, and what activities you spend the most time doing.

What is consuming your thoughts and time? Is it wise, or does it leave you distracted?

Whatever is consuming your mind and your schedule is an indicator of where you are heading in your spiritual life. Does that mean that your schedule will have a seven-hour block set aside for daily prayers? Not likely. But if your schedule is full of distractions and empty of any time spent reading your Bible, praying, and living in community with other Jesus-followers, it's time for a change.

Now What?

Passage to Study: Ephesians 5:1-20

Questions:
1. What takes up the most time and space in your schedule? Is it stoking your fire for Jesus?
2. When you get distracted and find your thoughts drifting, what do you think about? Would you categorize that as thoughts you should cling to or thoughts you should push away?

Week 4 – Day 2

James 4:14 – "Why, you do not even know what will happen tomorrow. What is your life? You are a mist that appears for a little while and then vanishes."

What is consuming your thoughts and time today?

Sometimes even thinking about *good* things can consume us and distract us from God. Let me explain.

Many people dwell too much on thoughts of tomorrow, next week, and next year – and none of those thoughts are evil. But such thinking can stop us from living in the present.

James was talking to people who were putting all their hope in what might happen in the future. While they waited for what may or may not happen, they became complacent during the present. James told these people that they didn't know for sure what would happen tomorrow, let alone a year or two from now.

As you think about and plan for your future, are you ignoring opportunities to serve Jesus *right now*? Planning for the future is not a sin; the Bible encourages it. But you aren't living out God's plan for your life if you fail to live today because you are waiting on tomorrow. Our life is like a mist – only here for a short period of time. How tragic would life be if we failed to live and be present in each day because we were waiting for the next?

Week 4 – Day 2 Applied

Upward – Focus on God
What does today's passage tell you about God's character, promises, plans, or heart?

What attitude or emotion should that spark in you?

Inward – Personal Application
What does this passage reveal about your habits, attitude, and heart?

Is there an attitude you need to change, action you need to take, or sin you need to turn from?

Outward – Live It Out
What is the next step you must take to live out the truth of today's passage?

When and how will you take that step?

Week 4 – Day 3

Romans 12:2 – "Do not conform to the pattern of this world, but be transformed by the renewing of your mind. Then you will be able to test and approve what God's will is—his good, pleasing and perfect will."

The goals of a Christian are often the opposite of cultural norms. This isn't a new thing; it has been happening since Jesus walked the earth. Christians have always lived counter to the present culture.

How do we continue to stoke our passions for Jesus in the midst of constant opposition from our culture?

Spiritual growth is based on daily decisions. We choose to live according to God's instructions for His people, or we don't. Romans 12:1-2 tells us that being a Jesus-follower means we follow with our whole life. We aren't perfect, but we are works in progress learning about Jesus and living out His teachings. Every day, you decide between the pattern the world lays out or the pattern God has established for you.

Paul gave us instructions as Jesus-followers to think about and act on the purposes of Jesus. He did that because you act on what you think about and you become what you repeatedly do. Actions begin as thoughts.

May your fire be stoked because your mind is focused on Jesus. If you focus your mind and thoughts on Jesus, you will stoke your spiritual fire without much effort.

Week 4 – Day 3 Applied

Upward – Focus on God
What does today's passage tell you about God's character, promises, plans, or heart?

What attitude or emotion should that spark in you?

Inward – Personal Application
What does this passage reveal about your habits, attitude, and heart?

Is there an attitude you need to change, action you need to take, or sin you need to turn from?

Outward – Live It Out
What is the next step you must take to live out the truth of today's passage?

When and how will you take that step?

Week 4 – Day 4

Proverbs 4:23 – "Above all else, guard your heart, for everything you do flows from it."

Imagine that you have an old car you would like to fix up. You can lift a car, you can redo the paint job, and you can install a nice sound system. The outside of the car may look incredible, but the car will break down all the time if you only fix the cosmetics and fail to maintain the engine.

We assume that if the outer appearance seems fine, our motives and intentions must be in check as well. But our hearts have a way of offering insight to what is really going on in our lives. When moments are full of emotions – stress, anger, confusion, etc. – we see what our lives of full of. Are we quick to blame others? Are we greedy? Do we watch out for ourselves and throw others under the bus for decisions we make? Are we driven by a desire to be popular rather than a desire to be godly?

As we studied yesterday, all actions start within us. Actions begin as ideas. Ideas begin as thoughts. Your thoughts are shaping your life. That is why it is imperative for you to guard your mind and heart.

Don't confuse learning to love God more with behavior modification. The outside of someone's life may look great – even godly. But if that individual's heart isn't guarded, they won't be able to stoke their fire for God. If that individual's inner life isn't focused on God, they will feel far from Him.

Week 4 – Day 4 Applied

Upward – Focus on God
What does today's passage tell you about God's character, promises, plans, or heart?

What attitude or emotion should that spark in you?

Inward – Personal Application
What does this passage reveal about your habits, attitude, and heart?

Is there an attitude you need to change, action you need to take, or sin you need to turn from?

Outward – Live It Out
What is the next step you must take to live out the truth of today's passage?

When and how will you take that step?

Week 4 – Day 5

1 John 1:8-9 – "If we claim to be without sin, we deceive ourselves and the truth is not in us. If we confess our sins, he is faithful and just and will forgive us our sins and purify us from all unrighteousness."

Sin is the most obvious cause for you to feel that your spiritual fire has fizzled or gone out completely. Christians know they have a sin problem. That's the first thing you need to understand to see your desperate need for Jesus.

Are you consistently confessing your sin to Jesus?

Ignoring your sin doesn't make it go away. Only the sacrifice of Jesus can cleanse you of your sin. The Bible is clear: Christians must confess their sins to Jesus and to other believers. Many believe the lie that if we hide or ignore sin, it will magically disappear when enough time has passed. In actuality, when we uncover our sin through confession, Jesus covers us with grace, mercy, and forgiveness.

We need to be in the habit of confessing our sins to keep sin from taking our minds captive.

One of the most important meetings of your day could be an evening conversation with Jesus about your day. How did you respond when there was adversity? Did you make Jesus known at your school today? Are there areas of sin that controlled you today? Confession can be as simple as grabbing your journal and Bible and praying through the events of your day.

Week 4 – Day 5 Applied

Upward – Focus on God
What does today's passage tell you about God's character, promises, plans, or heart?

What attitude or emotion should that spark in you?

Inward – Personal Application
What does this passage reveal about your habits, attitude, and heart?

Is there an attitude you need to change, action you need to take, or sin you need to turn from?

Outward – Live It Out
What is the next step you must take to live out the truth of today's passage?

When and how will you take that step?

Week 4 – Day 6

Philippians 4:8 – "Finally, brothers and sisters, whatever is true, whatever is noble, whatever is right, whatever is pure, whatever is lovely, whatever is admirable—if anything is excellent or praiseworthy—think about such things."

Have you ever watched a children's movie with a young kid only to hear jokes that aren't appropriate for kids? You may have even seen the movie before and not remembered any of those references.

How does that happen to us? Why do we forget that some of our favorite movies and television shows contain questionable jokes, language, and sexual scenes?

We become numb to inappropriate content because we allow it to enter our minds for hours each day. Between social media, shows, and music, your mind is flooded with hours of content every day. If there is no consideration about the quality of that content, you will become numb to it.

What do you spend your day thinking about? If we are honest, we don't give much thought to our thoughts. Paul told the church in Philippi to only allow noble, holy, admirable, and pure content to fill their minds and hearts. It is dangerous for Christians to become familiar with inappropriate content. This familiarity almost always suffocates your spiritual fires by leading you toward sin and away from Jesus.

Week 4 – Day 6 Applied

Upward – Focus on God
What does today's passage tell you about God's character, promises, plans, or heart?

What attitude or emotion should that spark in you?

Inward – Personal Application
What does this passage reveal about your habits, attitude, and heart?

Is there an attitude you need to change, action you need to take, or sin you need to turn from?

Outward – Live It Out
What is the next step you must take to live out the truth of today's passage?

When and how will you take that step?

WEEK 5

HOW HAS JESUS SHOWN UP IN MY LIFE THIS WEEK?

Week 5 – Day 1

How Has Jesus Shown Up in My Life This Week?

It is a miracle that I make it through each summer without buying a Jeep Wrangler or pop-up camper.

I don't own a camper or a Jeep. Those two items got bumped onto my "Next Purchases" list when I found out my wife was pregnant with our first child. Suddenly I was buying diapers and jokingly calling my son my camper because I knew it would be a long time before I would buy one!

But every year when the weather gets warm, I think about how nice it would be to own a Jeep or to go camping. And then I notice every Jeep on the road and every pop-up camper for sale on the side of the road. True story. I won't bring it to everyone's attention, but I see them driving along in their oversized mud tires. One day, during my normal twenty-minute commute to and from work, I noticed twelve Jeep Wranglers! Once I see a Jeep Wrangler, I can't help but notice them wherever I go. It doesn't matter if I want to buy one or not – I see Jeeps everywhere.

Seeing Jeeps and RVs reminds me of a few things:

I notice things I want to notice.
I notice what I'm thinking about.

I see what I'm looking for.

Does the Jeep dealership know I'm contemplating buying a Jeep and make an elaborate plan to place a Jeep on my route? Of course not. This isn't some creepy reality TV show with perfect product placement. It is my life.

Are there more Jeeps on the road in summer? Is the Jeep-per-crossover ratio swinging in favor of the 4x4 vehicle? Not at all.

My mind is the only thing that has changed. The more I think about Jeeps, the more I see them. It is as simple as that. I fix my eyes on Jeep Wranglers.

We notice things we are looking for. You might not want a Jeep Wrangler or a pop-up camper, but I'm sure you have had the same thing happen to you before. When your mind is focused on an item you want to buy, you begin seeing it all over the place.

New phones.
New clothes.
New cars.
New fast food restaurants.

It doesn't matter what it is, only that you are thinking about it. Once you have it on your mind, you notice it more when you see it.

Open Your Eyes to the Works of Jesus

It is interesting what we see when we start paying attention.

You find yourself noticing something because you have adjusted your attention. Our brains are wired to notice differences in our surroundings. It does this as a survival trick to make sure threats are dealt with before they hurt us. Many of us only notice negative things happening around us.

In order for us to keep the flames burning for Jesus, we need to notice how He is showing up in our lives. This is a reality we tend to forget. Jesus is working all around us. He is working through His people. Lives are being changed! Jesus-followers are serving others! Prayers are being answered!

The power of Jesus is moving! Do we notice it?

Unfortunately, most of us don't. We fail to notice Jesus' transformative work happening in our communities. Each day comes and goes without a realization that Jesus is moving. In John 5:17 Jesus makes it clear that God is always working: "... My Father is always at his work to this day, and I too am working." Jesus also taught about the Holy Spirit – God's presence on Earth and in His people. Jesus said that the work of the Holy Spirit was to teach, empower, encourage, remind us of Jesus' teachings, and intercede for us. (See John 14:26, Romans 8:26, and 1 Corinthians 2:6-16 for more information about the work of the Holy Spirit.)

If we are certain that God still moves, why can't we see Him working? Often it is because we aren't looking for evidence of Him transforming lives. Instead of looking for the ways God is working, we tend to think about negative situations. The evening news is a great example of this. Crime and scandal stories beat out uplifting news coverage all the time. If we aren't careful, we will do the same and become cynical in our outlook on life. We will always believe that the worst is going to happen and that people will never change.

Negative Thoughts Breed Negative Thoughts

Our cynicism and negativity can be reversed simply by looking for the ways God is at work around us. If we get in the habit of noticing the things God is up to, we are better able to handle the negative when it comes up. If we don't consciously look for the ways God is at work, all we will see is the negative. And the negative things will grow and grow until they are too big. We will stop noticing God at work at all, and we will grow in anger against God instead of passion for God.

There is one night of my childhood that perfectly illustrates this concept. One night after basketball practice in high school, I decided to rent a movie and watch it alone in my room. (Yes, it was a VHS. Yes, I got it from Blockbuster. I'm old, OK?)

The reason this night stands out to me is because I experienced something truly terrifying – and I'm not scared easily.

I sat down in my room to watch a scary movie. I don't remember which movie I was watching, but fourteen-year-old me was feeling a little bit of fear. My room was originally a screened-in porch that had been converted into a bedroom, so it had an exterior door. Halfway through the movie, I heard a noise at that door.

The noise was faint at first. It sounded like something or someone was standing by the door breathing heavily. Trying to keep my cool, I decided to ignore the noise and keep watching the movie.

Ten minutes later, I heard a noise again – the faint breathing of a person now accompanied by rustling leaves. This couldn't be happening! What are the odds a killer approaches my house while I'm watching a scary movie? I couldn't ignore the noise anymore. I stood up and slowly walked to the door to figure out what was outside.

Quiet footstep by quiet footstep, I approached the door and placed my ear against it. What happened next sent me into a panic. As my ear touched the door, something hit against it!

I lost it! There was obviously a killer trying to get into my room. In that moment, I deeply regretted playing basketball instead of taking martial arts. I ran upstairs and woke my parents up by yelling, "Someone is trying to kill me!" My panic rubbed off on them, and we all went downstairs to check it out.

My dad slowly opened the exterior door of my room ready to do battle with whatever was outside. As the door opened we finally caught a glimpse of the perpetrator. It was a raccoon.

I stacked a few boxes outside earlier in the week and forgot to take them to the trash. The raccoon was just searching for some food. He knocked all the boxes down, and they hit my door at the exact moment I placed my ear on it to listen for the "killer" outside.

Things Aren't Always as They Seem

Things aren't always as they seem, are they? The noise in our lives causes us to shift our attention away from the goodness of Jesus.

That night in high school when a raccoon made me almost wet myself from fear is an example of a time I was so caught up in noise that I wasn't able to see the truth.

Think about it. My mind was already primed to assume that the noise outside my room was a killer. I was watching a scary movie at the time the noise occurred!

The same thing happens to us as we approach our lives. If we are focused primarily on negativity, we have a hard time seeing that God is still at work and that He is for us.

We get caught up trying to find ourselves. For some, their main focus is trying to find themselves by saying yes to everything that comes their way. Your heart will not lead you to the best version of you. Only Jesus will complete you. Stop trying to find yourself and start understanding how God has gifted you.

We get caught up trying to find the one. Are you obsessed with finding someone to date? I'll let you in on a little secret – no spiritually mature Christian has ever said, "You know, I wish I started dating earlier in life and dated more people." Pursue righteousness before you pursue Mr. Right or you will settle for Mr. Right Now.

We get caught up trying to fit in with the popular crowd. While we are talking about relationships, which crowd are you pursuing? What are they known for? How are they perceived by others? Do they lead you closer to Jesus? Is your desire to find the acceptance of people to the detriment of your relationship with Jesus?

If, instead, we make it a habit to notice God at work, we will begin to see Him all around us. There is power in listing out how God has shown up in our lives in the past. We can list out the times He has intervened for us. We can try to count the number of prayers He has answered. We can list out the ways He has protected our friends and family members from danger or sickness.

When we direct our attention toward God, we can see and agree with Romans 8:28, which says, "And we know that in all things God works for the good of those who love him, who have been called according to his purpose." We will be able to look past the bad in our circumstances and see how God is at work even in hard times.

The author of Hebrews noticed that early Christians had a difficult time focusing on Jesus. Hebrews 12:1-2 says, "Therefore, since we are surrounded by such a great cloud of witnesses, let us throw off everything that hinders us and the sin that so easily entangles. And let us run with perseverance the race marked out for us, fixing our eyes on Jesus, the pioneer and perfecter of faith. For the joy set before him he endured the cross, scorning its shame, and sat down at the right hand of the throne of God."

Living out our faith has never been easy. It wasn't easy for the early Christians. Typically we think that was because of persecution. While it is true that the early Christians were persecuted, the writer of Hebrews doesn't mention persecution here.

The author of Hebrews listed two things the early Christians needed to remove – "everything that hinders" and "the sin that so easily entangles."

What was hindering the early Christians? Hebrews 12:2 use the imagery of running a race. And the first warning we see is to remove everything that hinders. Just so we are clear, runners do not carry weights during a race. They wear minimal clothing to decrease the weight of their clothes. Less weight gives the runner more energy to focus on running. And if you think our modern-day track uniforms are revealing, you should know that in the first century men raced in their birthday suits. Yup, men ran in the nude.

The author of Hebrews wasn't telling the early Christians to live out their faith in a nudist colony. The author wanted the early Christians to lay down any heavy things they carried in their minds and hearts to better focus on Christ.

How Has Jesus Shown Up in My Life This Week?

Nothing encourages us to live for Jesus like seeing Jesus transform lives. This question, "How has Jesus shown up in my life this week?" trains our minds to fix our attention on how Jesus is working.

Jesus is working in your life. Jesus will use anything and everything to get our attention. We can see Him move in our lives through reading an encouraging Bible verse at the perfect time. We see Jesus move in our lives when a close friend affirms an area of life we have been insecure about.

We see Jesus work in our lives through answered prayers. How many times have you prayed for safety before a road trip and arrived to your destination safely? Most of us fail to praise Jesus for smaller prayers He answers.

Don't miss this – Jesus is at work.

God never sleeps.
God never takes a vacation.
God is not absent.

Jesus is working in and through people to bring others to Himself. Nothing stokes our fire for Jesus like a fresh movement of Jesus' power in our lives. We notice the things that we think about. What we think about starts to show up in our lives. We see Jeep Wranglers, new phones, or the people that we hope will notice us. The same can be true about the work of Jesus. We will begin to see how Jesus is moving in our lives when we focus our attention on His power. Noticing Jesus' power in your life will fuel your praise and worship. Your passion for Jesus will burn brighter and hotter as you see His love and power transform lives.

Jesus is at work. Are you noticing how Jesus is working in your life?

Now What?

Passage to Study: Colossians 1:15-23

Questions:
1. When was the last time you were convinced something was true, only to find out that it wasn't?
2. How can you remind yourself of what Jesus has done and begin to notice what He is currently doing in your life? How is He working in the Christians around you?

Week 5 – Day 2

John 16:33 – "I have told you these things, so that in me you may have peace. In this world you will have trouble. But take heart! I have overcome the world."

Near the end of the book of John, Jesus began to predict His death, burial, and resurrection. To give the disciples encouragement, He said, "But take heart! I have overcome the world!"

How could the disciples have peace when Jesus would no longer be walking beside them? How would their questions be answered if Jesus wasn't with them? How would they have power to stand for what is honorable if their rock was gone?

Jesus didn't sugarcoat the truth – His followers will experience troubles and trials. Have you ever stood in a river? The power of flowing water rushes against your legs and makes it difficult for you to stand. It seems easier to lift your legs up and go with the flow. However, the powerful river will lead you away from where you need to be. The temptation for Christians is to lift our legs up and go with the flow of our culture. We are told to accept sin, ignore issues, and stay silent about spiritual topics. But if we do, we find ourselves slowly drifting away from where Jesus intends for us to be.

Jesus knows that we will face resistance as we take a stand, but He doesn't leave us to stand in our own power. Jesus has defeated death. We stand as victors, empowered by God's Holy Spirit working in our lives.

Week 5 – Day 2 Applied

Upward – Focus on God
What does today's passage tell you about God's character, promises, plans, or heart?

What attitude or emotion should that spark in you?

Inward – Personal Application
What does this passage reveal about your habits, attitude, and heart?

Is there an attitude you need to change, action you need to take, or sin you need to turn from?

Outward – Live It Out
What is the next step you must take to live out the truth of today's passage?

When and how will you take that step?

Week 5 – Day 3

Psalm 68:19 – "Praise be to the Lord, to God our Savior, who daily bears our burdens."

God carries the weight of your burdens and issues. He isn't frustrated by your weakness. He embraces you. You don't have to fear voicing your dependency on God. He already knows what you are struggling with. Take a few minutes today to journal.

Write out a recent time or situation in which you saw God move.

God, thank you for moving in my life by:

Write down something that is currently weighing you down.

God, you daily bear my burdens. Today, I need you to carry:

Week 5 – Day 3 Applied

Upward – Focus on God
What does today's passage tell you about God's character, promises, plans, or heart?

What attitude or emotion should that spark in you?

Inward – Personal Application
What does this passage reveal about your habits, attitude, and heart?

Is there an attitude you need to change, action you need to take, or sin you need to turn from?

Outward – Live It Out
What is the next step you must take to live out the truth of today's passage?

When and how will you take that step?

Week 5 – Day 4

Proverbs 3:5-6 – "Trust in the Lord with all your heart and lean not on your own understanding; in all your ways submit to him, and he will make your paths straight."

Have you ever been canoeing or kayaking? These small boats are a ton of fun in the water but can be difficult to balance. If you lean too far to the left or the right, you will tip over the canoe and be thrown into the lake!

Fixing our eyes on Jesus is the first step in trusting His leadership. We must rely on Jesus to make our paths straight because we aren't capable of doing it ourselves.

We don't see the future of what may happen in our lives. We can't make a perfect life plan because we don't have the perspective or knowledge that Jesus has. Leaning on our own understanding will always lead to us tipping over our boat and falling in the water.

Jesus brings stability to our lives. He keeps us from dangerous situations that will cause our passion to burn out. Sometimes Jesus shows up in our lives by protecting us from our own horrible decisions.

Week 5 – Day 4 Applied

Upward – Focus on God
What does today's passage tell you about God's character, promises, plans, or heart?

What attitude or emotion should that spark in you?

Inward – Personal Application
What does this passage reveal about your habits, attitude, and heart?

Is there an attitude you need to change, action you need to take, or sin you need to turn from?

Outward – Live It Out
What is the next step you must take to live out the truth of today's passage?

When and how will you take that step?

Week 5 – Day 5

Psalm 143:6 – "I spread out my hands to you; I thirst for you like a parched land."

When was the last time the power went off in your house? Nothing catches us off guard more than a power outage, unless you are a doomsday prepper. You stumble through the darkness trying to find a light. Each step is made with caution as you try to navigate the darkness. Sometimes you can't remember where the obstacles are in your own living room!

We need light to guide us in the darkness.

When dark times come, who are you reaching your hands out to for help? Your girlfriend? Your bank account? Your family? Don't be naive, dark times will come. Dark times creep in from our sinful decisions or from external situations. Like a parched land is waiting for the rains to come, we look to Jesus to move during the difficult times.

Jesus is the light of the world (John 8:12). He is our guide. The light of Jesus shines brightest in dark times. So we spread out our hands to Jesus alone, knowing that He is our security and strength.

Look for how Jesus has moved in the dark seasons of life.

Week 5 – Day 5 Applied

Upward – Focus on God
What does today's passage tell you about God's character, promises, plans, or heart?

What attitude or emotion should that spark in you?

Inward – Personal Application
What does this passage reveal about your habits, attitude, and heart?

Is there an attitude you need to change, action you need to take, or sin you need to turn from?

Outward – Live It Out
What is the next step you must take to live out the truth of today's passage?

When and how will you take that step?

Week 5 – Day 6

Psalm 46:10-11 – "He says, 'Be still, and know that I am God; I will be exalted among the nations, I will be exalted in the earth.' The Lord Almighty is with us; the God of Jacob is our fortress."

If you've ever ridden a roller coaster, you know that the ride doesn't always travel at top speed. In fact, the climb to the top of the ride is very slow.

As the roller coaster crawls to the top, you are able to survey the entire park. You can see people moving around, other rides, and talk with the person beside you. But once the roller coaster begins the steep descent, the speed of the ride limits your sight. You are moving too fast to see a clear picture of your surroundings. Everything passes by in a blur!

Rest is essential to noticing how Jesus is moving in and around your life. Busy schedules cause us to move too fast to notice what is going on around us. A busy schedule can burn out your fire for Jesus just as quickly as an addiction can. Being busy doesn't make you a better Christian. God tells us that we must be still and remember that God is God and we are not. Slowing the pace of our schedules allows us to see more of what God is doing around us. The Psalmist reminds us that God is always with us. Being still brings rest and helps us see how God is moving.

Week 5 – Day 6 Applied

Upward – Focus on God
What does today's passage tell you about God's character, promises, plans, or heart?

What attitude or emotion should that spark in you?

Inward – Personal Application
What does this passage reveal about your habits, attitude, and heart?

Is there an attitude you need to change, action you need to take, or sin you need to turn from?

Outward – Live It Out
What is the next step you must take to live out the truth of today's passage?

When and how will you take that step?

WEEK 6

WHO AM I BRINGING CLOSER TO JESUS?

Week 6 – Day 1

Who Am I Bringing Closer to Jesus?

I took the best field trip of my life in fifth grade. All the Safety Patrollers at my school were able to tour Washington, DC.

You read that correctly, I was in the Safety Patrol. Your school may have missed out on this fantastic public service managed by fifth graders, but my school didn't. We ensured the halls were safe and that younger kids made it safely into the building from the school bus. We were basically child versions of Ninja Turtles battling the Shredders of the community.

I haven't told you the best part. The Safety Patrol wore a brightly-colored safety patrol belt with a badge.

And I was part of the group.

Besides saving our community from crime, each year the Safety Patrollers took a trip to Washington, DC.

At the end of fifth grade, I loaded up my disposable cameras and prepaid pay phone calling cards, hopped in a tour bus, and journeyed eight hours to our country's capital.

We arrived in Washington, DC, early that afternoon. Our teacher, Miss Wells, gave us our room assignments and checked us into the hotel. There were a few dozen elementary schools who participated in this event.

My best friends roomed with me. Robert, Franky, Tony, and I packed out one small hotel room. There were not four cooler fifth grade guys on the planet.

Fifth Graders + Safety Patrol Badges = James Bond Level Coolness

We decided to turn in early that evening. I say "we decided" ... but there wasn't much of a choice. Miss Wells told all the students to head to their rooms and said the teachers were going to duct tape the door frames from the outside. This would tell them if any students left their rooms.

In the middle of the night, a dryer malfunctioned in the laundry room on the first floor and caught on fire.

The laundry room was located five doors from our room.

Luckily, the hotel had a ton of fire alarms that were in working order. The alarms started blaring and fifth graders started running out of the hotel.

It was a madhouse. Kids were running everywhere. Teachers were trying to gather their kids. Hotel staff were ensuring each school had every child accounted for.

Miss Wells began to count our fifth grade class. Then she counted a second time. Then a third. Each time she came up short.

She was missing four students. Four students who were still inside the hotel that was on fire.

Miss Wells gathered her composure and called roll to find out which four students she was missing.

Robert, Franky, Tony, and I were still inside the hotel.

Without hesitation, Miss Wells ran into the hotel to find us. She darted down our hallway to find it was filling with smoke.

Our door was still duct-taped. We were still inside. So she started beating on the door and yelling for us to wake up. Somehow, we hadn't woken up for the fire alarms going off inside our room or the flashing lights on the alarms. The duct tape sealed off the door, so the smoke didn't make it into the room.

Five minutes of beating on the door finally led to one of us waking up and checking the door. The four of us were standing in our pajamas outside in the cold parking lot before we knew it.

Miss Wells saved our lives.

We made it back to our rooms a few hours later once the fire department extinguished the fire in the laundry room.

Fires Draw People In

In the pursuit of stoking our own spiritual fires, it's easy to forget that other people need the love of Jesus to rescue them from the flames of destruction and sin. After all, we think about ourselves more than we think about any other person on this planet. It is easy to fall into a trap of focusing solely on our safety and neglecting to rescue those in need. Jesus-followers who have the strongest faith are often those who are bringing people closer to Jesus. The passion inside of strong Christians burns so brightly that they cannot help but stoke other people's spiritual fires.

Psalm 96:1-3 says this:

"Sing to the Lord a new song;
sing to the Lord, all the earth.
Sing to the Lord, praise his name;
proclaim his salvation day after day.
Declare his glory among the nations,
his marvelous deeds among all peoples."

This song has three distinct commands: sing, proclaim, and declare.

We are to sing about the goodness of God, proclaim that He has rescued us, and tell others about how God is searching for them as well. Jesus cares about your religious convictions *and* about your social concern.

See, a fire gives light to the surrounding area. People are attracted to the light. They come around a campfire for warmth and friendly conversation. Families gather around the fireplace to have conversations after dinner.

Fires have a way of bringing people in.

Your fire and passion for Jesus should have the same effect on those around you.

Jesus commands us to spread the truth about His love, mercy, grace, and forgiveness. We see this in the Great Commission (Matthew 28:18-20). We are to teach, proclaim, and make disciples as we go throughout our journeys.

This isn't reserved for pastors in the church or missionaries in foreign countries. This command is an expectation for every Jesus-follower to go out and bring other people closer to Jesus.

Every Jesus-follower must ask the question, "Who am I bringing closer to Jesus?"

Don't Miss an Opportunity

Who are the people you interact with on a daily basis? Do your interactions point to Jesus? Does your fire for Jesus bring warmth to others' lives?

If we aren't careful, we can pass by thousands of people each day and fail to point them to Jesus.

It's like the kitchen trash can during Thanksgiving. Everyone piles their plates into the can. The trash can starts to overflow with cups, plates, and the mystery meat your weird aunt brought. Instead of taking out the trash, what does everyone do? They keep adding trash onto the pile! Everyone knows where the trash bags are located. Anyone can tie the bag and walk it to the garage. But everyone adds plate after plate, waiting for someone else to take responsibility and meet the need.

Our community is in desperate need of the saving grace of Jesus. Our passion for Jesus must burn brightly to draw others to the source of our hope – Jesus.

When I think about this concept I'm reminded of a time I was serving at a church and one of our students wasn't at small group. One of the leaders noticed, and it got everyone asking about him.

"Where is Nick?"
"Has anyone seen him?"
"Nope. It's been weeks."

So the high school group leaders began asking other people in the church about Nick.

"Where has Nick been?"
"Where is Nick?"
"Is Nick mad?"

But no one picked up the phone to call Nick. He wasn't aware that anyone missed him because his leaders asked everyone about Nick ... except Nick.

If you are a Christian, you have an incredible commission from God to go and make disciples. Text. Go after people. Everyone belongs. Everyone needs to know who Jesus is and what He offers them.

Many Christians refuse to talk about spiritual matters with people who aren't already Christians. It might be awkward, they reason. Or it could be seen as confrontational.

In some ways, those arguments are true. As we discussed earlier, fires bring warmth and bring people in. But only if they are controlled. A controlled fire is useful and welcoming, but a wildfire brings devastation.

How you talk to other people about Jesus is extremely important.

1 Peter 3:15-16 reminds us: "But in your hearts revere Christ as Lord. Always be prepared to give an answer to everyone who asks you to give the reason for the hope that you have. But do this with gentleness and respect, keeping a clear conscience, so that those who speak maliciously against your good behavior in Christ may be ashamed of their slander."

We all need to be ready to share why we follow after Jesus. Our conversations must be seasoned with gentleness and respect.

Our words matter.
Our stories matter.
Our tone matters.
Our emotions matter.

Why? Because people matter to Jesus.

And if people matter to Jesus then they matter to His followers.

The Coldest Night of the Year

Have you ever had great intentions but failed to follow through with your idea? A few years ago, a friend of mine learned the importance of serving right when an opportunity presents itself.

Phil is a pastor with a heart for missions and serving others. He has made it a point to teach his three children the importance of serving others.

One night, Phil was watching the local news with his youngest child, Tyler. That winter evening was bringing the coldest temperatures of the year. The meteorologists talked of deadly wind-chill and record low temperatures. Tyler, up a little later than normal, sat in the living room watching the evening news.

Tyler looked over to his dad and asked, "Dad, so tonight is going to be the coldest night of the year?"

Phil looked back at his elementary-aged son and said, "That is what they say, sport."

Tyler turned his attention back to the TV. A few minutes later Tyler began to process the implications of a cold night.

"Dad," he said, "are there homeless people sleeping outside tonight?"

"Sadly, there are," Phil said.

Tyler responded, "Well, can we round up some of our blankets and jackets and hand them out to them since they are sleeping outside?"

Phil thought this was a great idea. It seemed like Tyler had been listening as Phil taught him about the importance of helping others. Talk about a proud dad moment!

Phil looked at Tyler and said, "That is a great idea! Let's gather some blankets and jackets first thing tomorrow morning."

Concerned, Tyler said, "But Dad *tonight* is the coldest night of the year."

Immediately convicted, Phil decided they would head out that evening. They gathered blankets and jackets from their house. They stopped by a fast-food restaurant and bought some hot chili. And they drove around handing out blankets, jackets, and warm meals. As they went, they shared the love of Jesus with their words and their actions.

Who Am I Bringing Closer to Jesus?

Bringing others to Jesus starts with us stepping into someone else's world – meeting their needs, having a conversation, or checking in on a friend. People can't afford for us to wait for a more convenient time to serve. The truth is, there is never a convenient time for us to serve others. Serving takes time, money, energy, and effort – all of which we are short on. If we wait, we will miss opportunities to bring others closer to Jesus and stoke their spiritual fires.

The Apostle Paul encourages us to continue serving, sharing, and loving in Galatians 6:9-10 by saying, "Let us not become weary in doing good, for at the proper time we will reap a harvest if we do not give up. Therefore, as we have opportunity, let us do good to all people, especially to those who belong to the family of believers."

May we not forget that we have been left on this planet to draw others to Jesus. Your purpose isn't to build a comfortable life but to bring the warmth, light, and power of Jesus to others.

Who are you bringing closer to Jesus?

Now What?

Passage to Study: Galatians 6:1-10

Questions:
1. Do you think it's easier to share non-spiritual information with others (the outcome of a game, a sale at your favorite store, etc.) than to talk about spiritual things? Why do you think that is?
2. Have you ever tried to share the Gospel with someone and your encounter turn out badly? What was bad about it, and how can you approach that situation differently next time?
3. What are some ways you can ensure you are serving others as needs arise?

Week 6 – Day 2

Matthew 28:19 – "Therefore go and make disciples of all nations, baptizing them in the name of the Father and of the Son and of the Holy Spirit."

This is the beginning of the Great Commission. A commission is an instruction given to a group of people. Here in Matthew 28, Jesus gave His disciples one final instruction before He ascended into Heaven – go and make disciples.

Some people get hung up on the word "go" in verse 19. They start to ask, "Where do I need to go?" "How should I get there?" "What do I need to do before I go?"

This word can be a bit confusing. Typically, we view "going" as a trip or a move to another region. We go on foreign mission trips. We go on vacation. We go away to college.

But here, Jesus uses the word in another way. "Go," in the original language, literally means "as you are going." The command is for Jesus-followers to share the Gospel of Jesus as we go about our day-to-day lives. This doesn't mean that we stop serving on mission trips – Jesus is clear that we are to "make disciples of all nations." Going isn't either/or, it is both/and. We commit to sharing the Gospel of Jesus with our community as we go about our day-to-day activities. We also commit to sharing the Gospel with other nations by going there or supporting others who go there.

Week 6 – Day 2 Applied

Upward – Focus on God
What does today's passage tell you about God's character, promises, plans, or heart?

What attitude or emotion should that spark in you?

Inward – Personal Application
What does this passage reveal about your habits, attitude, and heart?

Is there an attitude you need to change, action you need to take, or sin you need to turn from?

Outward – Live It Out
What is the next step you must take to live out the truth of today's passage?

When and how will you take that step?

Week 6 – Day 3

Ephesians 4:29 – "Do not let any unwholesome talk come out of your mouths, but only what is helpful for building others up according to their needs, that it may benefit those who listen."

We must not only do good, we must speak well to and of others.

Words have the incredible power to build people up or tear them down. "Sticks and stones may break my bones, but words will never hurt me" is a flat-out lie. Words have the power to start a national movement, encourage a friend at just the right time, or burn someone. Our words are often more powerful than our actions.

Bringing others closer to Jesus starts with the way that you talk to them and the way you talk about them. If you profess to worship the God of love, your words and actions better back that up.

Everyone needs encouragement. No one has ever said, "You know, I've been encouraged *too much* this week. I wish people would be a little less encouraging. I could use a great insult right now." People cannot be over-encouraged. Small words of encouragement can change someone's life.

Week 6 – Day 3 Applied

Upward – Focus on God
What does today's passage tell you about God's character, promises, plans, or heart?

What attitude or emotion should that spark in you?

Inward – Personal Application
What does this passage reveal about your habits, attitude, and heart?

Is there an attitude you need to change, action you need to take, or sin you need to turn from?

Outward – Live It Out
What is the next step you must take to live out the truth of today's passage?

When and how will you take that step?

Week 6 – Day 4

John 13:34-35 – "A new command I give you: Love one another. As I have loved you, so you must love one another. By this everyone will know that you are my disciples, if you love one another."

What are Christians known for in your community? Are they known for their service, their arguing, or hypocrisy? Perhaps they are known for the things they are against. People, both inside and outside of the church, have varying definitions of what it means to be a Christian. Jesus said people will know we belong to Him by the way that we love one another.

So, what did Jesus' love look like?

Jesus' love is patient.
Jesus' love is fearless.
Jesus' love is forgiving.
Jesus' love is available.
Jesus' love is unrelenting.
Jesus' love is unchanging.
Jesus' love is unconditional.
Jesus' love is compassionate.

We will be known as Jesus-followers when we love others in these ways.

Week 6 – Day 4 Applied

Upward – Focus on God
What does today's passage tell you about God's character, promises, plans, or heart?

What attitude or emotion should that spark in you?

Inward – Personal Application
What does this passage reveal about your habits, attitude, and heart?

Is there an attitude you need to change, action you need to take, or sin you need to turn from?

Outward – Live It Out
What is the next step you must take to live out the truth of today's passage?

When and how will you take that step?

Week 6 – Day 5

Mark 10:45 – "For even the Son of Man did not come to be served, but to serve, and to give his life as a ransom for many."

Have you ever considered the absurdity of the Gospel? The King of the universe came on a rescue mission, leaving His rightful place in Heaven to walk among sinners. Jesus slept on the ground, endured the elements, and, not to be too crude, even had to use the restroom outdoors. He also endured hate, negativity, and backlash.

Jesus didn't come to earth looking to stay at a resort. He didn't come to make a few social appearances then retreat to the comfort of His large house. Jesus didn't eat expensive meals while He was on the road. Jesus didn't come to be served, although He is the One who deserves our praise and service! The King of the universe was finally on earth. But instead of being served, He served the despised, low, and broken.

It is tempting for us to believe that we have finally "arrived" during different seasons of life. The high school senior feels entitled to a few perks. The new boss wants everyone to help him carry the workload. Our culture thrives on self-serving motives.

This example is laid before every Jesus-follower. Christians, our earthly success is defined by how many people we serve, not by how many people serve us. The King of the universe came to serve. How are you serving and bringing others closer to Jesus?

Week 6 – Day 5 Applied

Upward – Focus on God
What does today's passage tell you about God's character, promises, plans, or heart?

What attitude or emotion should that spark in you?

Inward – Personal Application
What does this passage reveal about your habits, attitude, and heart?

Is there an attitude you need to change, action you need to take, or sin you need to turn from?

Outward – Live It Out
What is the next step you must take to live out the truth of today's passage?

When and how will you take that step?

Week 6 – Day 6

Galatians 6:9 – "Let us not become weary in doing good, for at the proper time we will reap a harvest if we do not give up."

Doing good is exhausting. In Galatians 6:9 the Apostle Paul encouraged the church in Galatia to continue doing what Jesus had commanded. He said, "... for at the proper time we will reap a harvest if we do not give up." Paul was describing a farmer who tends his garden. A good farmer will work in the fields every day planting, weeding, and watering to cultivate a crop. Crops, regardless of which type, do not shoot up overnight. A farmer works long hours with little proof that the crop is growing. He continues to work knowing that his work is leading to growth, *even if he can't see it*.

Bringing others closer to Jesus is the same. When needed, we share the Gospel, encourage, invite, have difficult conversations, give our time, invest our money, and lend a helping hand. At the end of the day, it is hard to see the spiritual growth of the people you are serving.

1 Corinthians 3:7 says, "So neither the one who plants nor the one who waters is anything, but only God, who makes things grow." God is the only one responsible for growth in your church and groups. God makes things grow. His followers work to bring others to Jesus, regardless of the visible, immediate results. So don't grow tired of serving and doing good – God is working in ways that we cannot see.

Week 6 – Day 6 Applied

Upward – Focus on God
What does today's passage tell you about God's character, promises, plans, or heart?

What attitude or emotion should that spark in you?

Inward – Personal Application
What does this passage reveal about your habits, attitude, and heart?

Is there an attitude you need to change, action you need to take, or sin you need to turn from?

Outward – Live It Out
What is the next step you must take to live out the truth of today's passage?

When and how will you take that step?

Continue to Fan the Flame

2 Timothy 1:6 – "For this reason I remind you to fan into flame the gift of God, which is in you through the laying on of my hands."

Fires go out when they are left alone.

You don't have to wait for another event to stoke your passion for Jesus – your fire can burn brightly today! It is my prayer that these six weeks have transformed your relationship with Jesus and empowered you to stoke your passion for Him.

God has a purpose for your life. Fires go out when they are left alone. Don't neglect your spiritual fire! Instead, keep stoking your fire for Jesus.

If you are looking for more ways to stoke your passion for Jesus, follow Chase's blog for weekly articles and encouragements to help you apply the Bible to your life.

www.ChaseSnyder.blog

About the Author

Chase Snyder is a Tennessee native living in Metro Atlanta, where he serves as the High School and Young Adults Pastor at FBC Loganville. While in Tennessee, he served at a few non-profits, including a Christian camp. There, he served more than 60,000 students and adults and ate approximately 200,000 hot dogs.

He is the founder of Ministry Bubble LLC, a ministry that produces books, blogs, and studies to help people apply the Bible to their daily lives.

He is the author of three books: *Stoked*, *Doer: Becoming a Christian Who Acts In A Passive Culture,* and *Doer Of God's Word: A 30 Day Devotional For Students*. He also writes downloadable studies for youth ministries.

Chase and his wife Anne have two kids, Tripp and Brooke. Chase loves camping, reading, kayaking, playing Go Fish with his kids, Bigfoot conspiracies, and Chemex coffee.

Connect with Chase

Twitter & Instagram: @ChaseSnyder12
Facebook: /ChaseSnyder12
Blog: www.ChaseSnyder.blog
Website: www.MinistryBubble.com

Additional Resources from Chase

Doer: Becoming A Christian Who Acts In A Passive Culture

Available on Amazon

Additional Resources from Chase

Doer of God's Word: A 30 Day Devotion For Students

Available on Amazon

Additional Resources from Chase

Doer – A 3-Session Retreat Study

Available on www.ChaseSnyder.blog

Additional Resources from Chase

180: Radically Changed – A 4-Session Retreat Study

Available on www.ChaseSnyder.blog

www.ingramcontent.com/pod-product-compliance
Lightning Source LLC
LaVergne TN
LVHW051523070426
835507LV00023B/3262